Transforming

Inspiring Stories & Powerful Tools for Manifesting Peace, Hope & Healing

Vol.1 in the Series: *We are Rising*

Special __FREE__ Bonus Gift for You

To help you to on your journey of transformation to become the human

you came here to be and

achieve more success in all your life circles

FREE BONUS ONLINE SUMMIT

for you at:

https://risesummits.com/transform-trauma/

3o in-depth training videos featuring the best in the world on how to

transform trauma

The R.I.S.E Movement®

Special Quantity Discounts

To Place an Order Contact:

orders@therisemovement.org

MOTIVATE AND

INSPIRE OTHERS

"Share This Book"

Retail $19.95
5-20 Books $16.95
21-99 Books $14.95
100-499 Books $12.95
500-999 Books $9.95
1,000+ Books $7.95

What Others Are Saying About The RISE Summit

Get your **FREE** Access here:
https://risesummits.com/transform-trauma/

"I found this course to be a fabulous source of personally helpful information. I was reluctant to do the course feeling like I had done enough work in these areas already. I am so happy I chose to do it. I have been able to use the processes to work through much of my residual childhood trauma in an easy comfortable manner. I am beyond grateful for all Nunaisi and her colleagues offered. Thank you is just to little to express myself. I feel like a new person."
~ Carol Kalf
*****

"Nuna Isi Your passion for healing and rising above is infectious. This was a wonderful, informative summit. I especially resonated with Hale Dwoskin. I may look him up in Sedona. I am looking forward to the release of the book ! "
~ Deborah Levine
*****

"Thank you Nuna Isi Ma for your beautiful creation, facilitation and presence for this Summit on what is the most pressing matter for humanity at this time. I am in awe of you and all your wonderful presenters. Sending

much love and blessings"
~ Andrew Solomon
*****

*"I loved this summit. Had some great speakers and
information about healing from past trauma."*
~ Marilee
*****

*"I have attended many summits and you did a great job
putting it all together. Including the gifts each speaker
had for the audience. I really liked the format the talk
and the gifts below in the same page. Many summit host
they have a separate link for the information or gifts
from the speaker and it can be confusing. Yours was
straight forward and well organised and educational.
Great selection of speakers. Love it!! Thank you for all
the work you are doing in the world.
Humanity needs this right now."*
~ Maria
*****

*"You held a very warm space. I thought you were really
good as the host and your questions were always so
clear. And you did not digress from your message."*
~ Kaytlyn
*****

*"It was eye opening and informative! Absolutely
amazing!"*
~ Luann
*****

"I enjoyed the summit very much. It was enlightening

and heart warming. Would have purchased the series if I had a better income. Thank you very much!"

~ Vanessa

*****

"Love your sharing at the end of the Summit. I can feel your passion and see your good work in the people you have worked with. Keep up with the spirit! Love."

~ Cindy

*****

"It was extremely interesting, the quality of the speakers, their interventions amazed me."

~ Vanessa Rousselle

*****

"I really appreciated this event happening and loved the title RISE, Thank you most kindly . I especially enjoyed Hale Dwoskins very simple technique with easy questions so our feelings, thoughts , situations , motives and the personal sense of, can be noticed from within , rather that suppress and resist ! Wonderful series all round ! Kind thanks again !!"

~ Kate Burke

*****

"The R.I.S.E. summit was so empowering when Dr. Ray spoke of doing somatic healing and not just talk therapy. This was transformative me after a rape I went through in 2018. I am so inspired to keep healing and release residual shame."

~ K Lorrie

*****

"You warm my heart just by existing and being you. I am a shattered woman, and the love you are pouring out with . this series is profoundly healing for me. For at least the hour that I listen, I am not in agony and I am reminded of the existence of the goodness of femininity."
~ Jodi S
*****

"Thank you for this wonderful journey- so happy to see all this beautiful woman- doing their sacred work. Thank you for sharing this wisdom with the people- and for you wonderful rise summit- many people will have a lot of good inspirations. Lots of Love to all of you."
~ Andrea Zen
*****

"Dear Nuna Isi, thank you so much for your work and all Those precious Impulses that "Rise" left Behind to continue my work... Blessings to you!"
~ Katharina Fuchs

REMEMBER·INSPIRE·SHARE·ELEVATE

It is Our Sacred Mission to Support at Least One Million People
to RISE to Their Full Potential
R.I.S.E stands for
Remember
Why you Came Here;
You have a Soul Purpose and a Sacred Mission that
Only You Can Bring into the World
Inspire
Others by Being Yourself;
Authentic and Vulnerable, Human and Divine
Share
Your Story and Your Heart;
The Wisdom you Gained through Your Life Journey is Gold
Elevate
Others to RISE

No More Time to Wait

More Postponing and You'll Be Late

It's Not a Rehearsal, Dear

Remember Why you Came Here

Stop Playing Small

Take off Your Mask Once and for All

Bring Your Anger, Rage and Pain

Let it Transform into Your Gain

Allow the Light Shine into your Scars

You Made From the Earth, Sun, Moon & Stars

Forget What You've Been Told

Be True, Be You, Be Bold

You are a King or Queen Among Kings and Queens

Ditch Competition, You have Your Unique Wins

So Step into Your Kingdom and Claim Your Crown

Don't Let Others Bring You Down

You are Magnificent, Human and Divine

All You Need is to Align

Your Voice is Vital; Your Insights are Gold

You Have Magic to Share with the World

Switch Yourself On and Turn the Volume Up

But Remember, First Fill Your Own Cup

~ Nunaisi Ma

This Book is Dedicated to
All our Children
From Whom we Borrow
This Planet Earth

Table of contents:

Lion Goodman

Lion Goodman is a professional certified Transformational Coach, Author, and Teacher. He developed the *Clear Beliefs Method* for permanently deleting limiting beliefs and healing core wounds from the psyche. More than 500 Coaches, Therapists, and Healers from around the world have graduated from his *Clear Belief Coach Training*, accredited by the International Coach Federation and the Association for Coaching. Find out more at http:// *www.ClearBeliefs.com* and http://www.LionGoodman.com.

"Every moment that you suppress or hold back the light that you are, you rob the world of the precious gift only you can give."
~ Lion Goodman

Clear the Way for Your Divine Light to Shine

As a child, I thought there was something wrong with me. I felt so different from other kids. I tried to figure out why they did what they did, and how they made friends so effortlessly. It appeared that I thought about myself much more than they thought about themselves. I felt separate and alone, so I became an observer of others. Maybe if I could be like them I would feel more comfortable in my skin. It was clear that there was something wrong with me. I began to look for ways to fix myself. Thus began my 55-year long journey of self-development.

At age 13, I discovered books on psychic phenomena and extra-sensory perception. My girlfriend and I practiced telepathy, psychometry, psychic projection and psychokinesis. I never made anything move with my mind, but I became really good at reading people.

I read everything I could about the mind and psychology. I joined groups, studied with teachers, practiced different disciplines such as yoga and meditation, and over the years attended more than 100 workshops and trainings. I studied the major religions of the world, philosophy, the sciences, and neurology. I took drugs and practiced shamanism. I was a consciousness explorer, searching for answers to the big questions: Who am I? What am I here for? What is life? I wanted to understand myself, others, and the world. There was a sense of adventure and joy as I learned more about myself, my purpose, and how to love.

After multiple revelations over a period of many years, I came to the conclusion that I knew *enough* to share the wisdom I had gathered with others.

Now, decades later, I operate a worldwide educational institution, training people from around the world how to clear beliefs and heal trauma.

Most people think of beliefs as a mental construct: "I believe in

God," or "I don't believe in God," or "I believe in less government" or "I believe in my own personal power." These are ideas you can put into a sentence, and decide, "I don't want to believe that anymore. I want to believe *this* instead." Through my 5 decades of research, I discovered that beliefs are the infrastructure of the human mind. They're what the mind is made of – in the same way that neurons are what the brain is made of.

We can observe our own human experience and recognise that it is multidimensional. Every experience we have includes vision, hearing, touch, sensing, thinking, planning, remembering, feeling, knowing, and being. They are all occurring at once, even though our conscious attention is more narrow. Although we talk about those aspects of experience as separate things that can be observed or manipulated, this is a function of how our mind is structured. It is designed to separate and make distinctions. It naturally reifies everything around us (to reify is to turn processes, events and states of affairs into a thing, or object).

We are whole, integrated beings, and yet we are also composed of parts. You can focus your attention on the whole, but the mind naturally tends to focus on parts. Of course, every whole is a part of another larger whole. We are part of, and connected to, our physical environment, social environment, cultural environment, family environment, etc.

We are multidimensional beings having multidimensional experiences. Beliefs can be thought of as conclusions that you come to from your experiences. That conclusion, or belief, must be multidimensional, as well.

Our beliefs are not merely mental constructs, but rather complex multidimensional aspects of our Whole Self. They are mental, emotional, physical, and spiritual. They include information from all of our senses, our connections to other people, and our experience of the world. Why is this important? Because our beliefs create and shape our reality. And if we want to change our reality, we have to change our beliefs.

We begin to form these conclusions from our earliest experiences, and patterns we notice around us. Even before we have words, we may conclude, "When that person comes close, I feel warm and cared for. When that other person comes close, I feel uncomfortable and cold."

Jeremy Lent calls this our "patterning instinct" in his brilliant book of the same name. This is how all animals survive in their world. They either have instincts, which are built-in biological beliefs, or they engage in some form of learning from elders and group members, or both. If the right patterns are latched onto and used to guide their behavior, they survive. What we call learning is the accumulation of beliefs: what I must do to survive. It developed over millions of years of evolution. The individuals who learned the most survived and produced the next generation. The learned patterns worked to ensure survival - both of the individuals and the group.

Our own belief system works to ensure our own survival. For example, a baby may conclude, from its experience, "If I cry and make a fuss, I'll get my needs cared for." This isn't a verbal conclusion, but rather an experiential one. This is a very good conclusion for that particular baby. It results in their survival. Another baby raised in a different environment may conclude, "If I stay quiet and don't make a fuss, I'll get my needs cared for."

Most of our *core* beliefs were established during our childhood, and they worked well for us - we survived! The problem is that most of those old beliefs don't work for us as adults. You may know one or two adults who still use the behavioural strategy, "If I cry and make a fuss, I'll get my needs met." In an adult, this belief produces unseemly behavior. The individual appears to be immature because their Human Operating System is still based on that immature belief.

Unfortunately, our old beliefs don't automatically expire and disappear. New beliefs simply get added on top of the old ones, and the old ones get pushed down into the subconscious mind. This is why our old patterns are so difficult to change. There are dozens of techniques for changing beliefs, but most of them are attempting to change them at the mental level. They haven't involved the subconscious mind or the superconscious mind. They may successfully change the mental body, but they ignore the emotional body, the physical body, and the spiritual body. Those early patterns are sticky because they were accumulated in order to survive. The mind thinks that they're still needed to continue to survive. They served us in our childhood, so they continue to echo throughout our lives, and at times they jump up and take over.

The only way to delete or change a multidimensional belief is to change it multidimensionally.

Once I recognized the central role beliefs play in creating our reality, I explored as many different methods of belief change as I could find. Most of them didn't work very well. The results were temporary or partial. You may have had the same experience. The clearest example is Affirmations and the so-called Law of Attraction. The theory is that if you think the right thoughts, and say affirmations enough times, things will change and a bag of money will fall into your lap. (I'm only slightly exaggerating…) If you've ever said affirmations, you probably noticed that you felt better for a while – 20 minutes to a couple of hours. Then you're right back to where you were before. So you say them even more. And then eventually, you give up, because for most people, nothing happens.

The same thing can happen in psychotherapy. You may have had one or two big realisations, but most hours you are just grinding away at the same problem set. Talk therapy doesn't produce the kind of radical change most of us are looking for.

I took all of this information and crafted a system of trauma-informed therapeutic coaching that produces deep and profound change rapidly and permanently. The Clear Beliefs Method is based on these fundamental understandings of consciousness, the mind, and how beliefs function. Our aim is to create change at the infrastructural layer that our mind is made of. This is far below the surface of the conscious mind, below the story-telling level. It works at the meaning-making level, the programming that forms our Human Operating System. When a shift happens here, it's equivalent to a revelation. The entire mind, body, emotions, and spirit changes. The transformation is profound, comprehensive, and permanent. You suddenly see the world differently, because the belief-lens you've been looking through has been changed, and so has everything around you.

Our beliefs act like selective filters for our perceptions. We believe that we're seeing reality, but we're seeing a tinted, shaped version. They allow us to perceive what we *believe*, and they filter out what we can't believe. For example, if you believe, "Life is hard," you can see how hard life is all around you. If you believe, "Life is joy," you see joy wherever you look. Beliefs are always self-reinforcing. We see evidence for our beliefs everywhere. Have you ever tried to argue with someone who had very fixed beliefs about a particular topic, such as politics, foreigners, abortion, or the environment? You know how unsuccessful that can be. A person with fixed beliefs (about any topic) cannot be persuaded to change their beliefs based on evidence, facts, or authoritative experts. Research has shown that when you present facts that challenge a person's belief, they don't adjust for the facts – they dig their heels in deeper and make your evidence wrong. This is referred to as "closed mindset" versus an "open mindset." However, when you change your belief filter at the infrastructure level, you see a different world and new possibilities. The old viewpoint about the topic has changed. A new viewpoint brings in new patterns of behavior, new ways of relating to people, a new "you."

The first step in any process of change is to increase awareness. When it comes to changing your beliefs, here is an exercise that begins the process. Let's use this example: you notice that there's something in the way of enjoying your sexuality, and you recognise that there must be some beliefs that are holding you back. You know that sexuality is one of our human needs that, when fulfilled, make us a more complete and joyful human being. Ready to begin the deep dive into your beliefs?

Think of this exercise as an excavation process. You're going to explore your beliefs using a trick of the mind Begin by saying to yourself, either out loud or silently, "Something I believe about sex is…" Then relax and let your mind finish the sentence. Whatever appears is a beliefs you have somewhere in you subconscious or conscious mind. You may hear, "Sex is dirty." You may or may not have known that this belief was inside of you. It may have been said to you once when you were a child, and it got buried deep in your subconscious mind. Later in life, you may have learned that sex is good clean fun, or an aspect of deep and intimate love. The old beliefs you had accumulated now buried deep. This exercise brings them back up to the surface.

Whatever comes up, write it down. Then say, "Another thing I believe about sex is... and write down whatever comes up next as a thought, feeling, or inner voice. You may hear, "Sex is wonderful." Write it down. Then say again, "Another thing I believe about sex is... " and you may hear, "It's hard to get it right." Write every thought down without judging it, countering it, or discarding it with, "I don't believe that!" If you hear a counter belief, doubt, or judgement, that's just that belief to write down, and repeat the prompt. Keep repeating the pattern over and over. You may write down 30, 50, or 100+ belief statements. The longer you do the exercise, the more subconscious beliefs will come up. Continue until your mind is completely quiet and doesn't have any other responses, or you start getting repeat answers.

Then move to a different topic: beliefs about relationships, or money, or work, or love, or friends, or family, or life, or death, or God. When your mind speaks, it's a good time to listen.

When you look at your lists of beliefs, you may be surprised at the volume of beliefs you carry. You've been accumulating beliefs and adding them to the pile throughout your life, and without knowing it. You've gotten programmed by parents, teachers, religious authorities, your culture, your friends, and the media in all of its forms. Plus you came to your own conclusions based on your own experiences. My best guess is that we have tens of thousands to hundreds of thousands of beliefs stored in our subconscious mind.

When you think about clearing your old beliefs, this appears to be an enormous and daunting task – but the good news is that you don't have to clear all of your beliefs. You only have to clear the ones that are interfering with your life in some way. Beliefs come in all flavours, and they produce a wide variety of impact on your life. Some beliefs are helpful, some are empowering, and many are neutral. Others are limiting, negative, interfering, or destructive. Here's an example of a helpful belief: "Look both ways before you cross the street." That's a good belief to have whether you're a child or an adult. It keeps you safe. Here's a destructive belief: "There's something so broken in me that I can't be repaired." That belief can take you down a really dark road.

Focus on clearing your limiting, negative, and problematic beliefs, and you will create a new and open space in front of you. New possibilities will appear. If you walk around with the belief, "No one is going to love me", or "I'm unlovable," it will be impossible to perceive the love that people have for you. Whenever you clear a belief, you create a space in which a new belief can be planted. The new one will grow and blossom just as the old one did. For example, if you clear that belief about being unlovable, and replace it with, "I am loved, I am loving, and I am love itself," others will perceive you differently, because you will be radiating a different energy. You will naturally perceive the love of others, and be able to love others. When a person who loves deeply walks into the room, you are immediately attracted to them. They're filled with a kind of light or glow you can feel. When you have that belief at your core, you will become naturally attractive to others..

After discovering your beliefs about a particular topic, go through the list and label them appropriately: neutral, positive, empowering, negative, interfering, destructive, etc. This step ensures that you will be more aware of them when they arise in the background of your mind. This awareness provides you a new option: you can decide whether to continue believing it, or not. There are many ways to disrupt the automatic nature of beliefs. One of the best is Byron Katie's "The Work." She invites you to ask these questions about your belief:

1. Is it true?
2. Can you absolutely know it's true?
3. How do you react (or feel) when you believe that thought?, and
4. Who would you be without that thought?

You then do what she calls a "turnaround." You try out as many different opposites of the original belief as you can. Here are examples of turnarounds to the belief, "I'm unlovable:"

1. I'm lovable.
2. You're unlovable.
3. They're all unlovable.
4. No one is unlovable.
5. I'm not able to express the love that I have.
6. Other people are not able to express their love for me.

Keep going, and saying each opposite belief out loud. Eventually, the original belief will become less powerful, or meaningless, or "just a belief." Other possibilities will open up.

Here's the limitation of this technique (and other similar techniques): they work at the level of the conscious mind, and they use language. The conscious verbal mind is one aspect of our human nature, but there are many other dimensions to human consciousness. Beliefs are stored in all dimensions at once. This technique does not involve the subconscious mind or the superconscious mind. (The question, "Who would you be without this belief?" can sometimes function as a stimulus into the spiritual dimension).

To clear a belief completely, you need to involve all aspects and all dimensions of the Self, not just one or two. The belief may have been formed out of one or more experiences, which are stored in the memory dimension. Beliefs are also stored in the dimension of feelings, and those feelings must be present to be cleared at the same time. Many of our deepest beliefs were formed before we had words, so they are stored in non-verbal memory, and verbal processes can't touch them (which is why talk therapy has limited value as a route to change). Words and language are abstraction-labels we use to point to particular things and feelings. The word "anxious" is pointing to a set of sensations in the body, but the word is not the sensation itself. Without direct awareness of the actual felt emotion, the belief can't be cleared completely.

The Clear Beliefs Method includes all aspects of experience, and all dimensions of the Self. Here's an experiment to try to experience the connection between beliefs and feelings: Close your eyes for a minute and feel what it feels like to hold the belief, "There's something wrong with me." You have many other beliefs that will come up and tell you that it's not true, but put those aside for this minute. Say it to yourself, and feel what it feels like as if you believed it 100%. Really FEEL it. Then let it go.

Most people feel some combination of heaviness, shame, their head lowers, posture collapses, or they have a sense of withdrawing into a shell to hide, or the urge to run away. Did you experience anything like that? Each person feels it in their own unique way – these are just the most common sensations.

Now, close your eyes and feel what it feels like to hold the belief, "I am a sacred and worthy being." Feel it as if this statement is 100% true. What does that feel like? Everyone will have a slightly different experience, but the most common feelings include a sense of lightness or lightening up, expansiveness, and an uplifting of the posture and deeper breath.

Our beliefs create feelings and sensations, either at the conscious level, or subtly in the background of our mind or feelings. Somatic Therapies focus on this embodied felt sense, and this is an important component of the underlying belief structure – so we include it in our work. However, when you focus ONLY on the somatic sense, you will also create a partial or temporary solution.

By attending to ALL aspects of human experience, we are able to clear the belief matrix completely. When that happens, it's immediately obvious at the felt sense level. It's gone. The heaviness has disappeared. The world looks different. The belief doesn't come back. This is my "acid test" for any belief-change or therapeutic technique: Does it disappear the beliefs completely? Is it permanent? Did the old belief sneak back in the back door? I am in support of any process or technique that produces complete and permanent results. There just aren't very many that do.

Our final step of the belief clearing process involves a guided imagery journey in which all aspects of the Self combine to delete the belief at all levels of consciousness. It involves memories, imagination, metaphors, visualisation, feelings, thoughts, emotions, and the True Self (or higher self). When the clearing process is complete, you know it. The old belief and its associated feelings are gone. It is no longer in consciousness. Many clients ask us, "What was my old belief again? I can't remember it." That's how completely gone it is.

In this new clear space, you can choose a new belief to replace the old one. Pick one that is empowering, positive, and enlightening. Think about creating a new garden. The first thing you do is clear the rocks and weeds out of the soil, turn the soil over and amend it. Then plant the seeds. They have the space, and what they need, to grow, blossom, and bear flowers and fruit for your life. If you throw seeds on rocky, weedy ground, nothing much will grow. This is why affirmations don't work. You're throwing new beliefs onto the rocky weedy ground of your old beliefs. This is why you're told to say the affirmation repeatedly. But it rarely works. Every once in a while, a flower grows. But you could have had an entire garden. Instead, clear the ground once, completely. Plant your seeds once in fertile ground. You don't need to do it over and over again.

In the *Clear Beliefs Coach Training*, I teach 15 different methods for finding and clearing core beliefs. Why? Because every person is unique. They have different experiences and different needs. When you have one technique that you apply to everyone, it's like trying to fix a car with just one wrench. (When all you have is a hammer, everything looks like a nail.) Most trainings in the coaching and healing professions offer one way to clear beliefs from the psyche. One wrench for everyone. Every technique will work for some people, some of the time. But not for most people most of the time.

Because the Clear Beliefs Method is based on these fundamental principles of how the mind and brain work, and on an understanding of who we are as unique souls, each with our own internal belief structure, we offer our students a complete tool set – the kind that a handyman brings to fix things at your house. She brings a complete set of tools because she doesn't know what the problems are in advance. She is prepared to meet almost any challenge.

The Clear Beliefs Method can be applied not only to clearing beliefs, but also clearing the adverse childhood experiences, traumas, psychological wounds, and adaptive strategies that occurred along with the belief itself. Most people have had one form of trauma or another. The trauma happened – we can't change that – bue we can change the conclusion that the child came to when it happened, the meaning they made of it, and the beliefs and strategies that resulted from doing so.

Trauma is not just something that happened *to you.* Sometimes it's what *didn't* happen *for you.* There are many forms of trauma other than the physical or shock trauma that we usually think of, such as attachment trauma, developmental trauma, birth trauma, intergenerational trauma, and cultural or societal trauma. There's a lot going on inside the human psyche! We need to dive as deeply as we can, find the source material, and clear it from the subconscious infrastructure where it is stored.

Here's an example of attachment trauma from my own life: my mother was good at the mechanical duties she was responsible for. She provided food, changed our diapers, clothed and sheltered us. We never wanted for anything – except a connection with her. Because she wasn't connected to herself, she couldn't connect with us as children. I felt like an object that was being moved around and shaped to her needs and desires, not a person with an independent consciousness, worthy of love and respect. This left me disconnected and lonely. I didn't learn how to form secure attachments with others – until I cleared that trauma. All children have the same needs: to be seen, heard, regarded as a person, held, nurtured, loved, connected and safe. This "hole in my soul" set me off on the path of healing and personal development. That was my adaptive strategy. Every person finds their way to deal with their trauma. Some are successful strategies, such as being perfect, becoming popular, or winning contests. Others choose unsuccessful adaptive strategies because of the wound – isolation, criminality, addictions, or gaining power over others.

When you clear the source of the adaptive strategy, the adaptive strategy is no longer useful, and it falls away.

There are many things that can interfere with our creating the life we want. It may be a subconscious belief, a series of traumas, negative internal voices, or a lack of connection to ourselves or others. Most failures occur not from the circumstances, but from quitting when the going gets tough. We are creators, and almost anything is possible if you put enough intention and attention on attaining it. However, our internal blocks, barriers and resistance can take us down, distract us, or convince us that we're not worthy of the prize. All of these limitations are based on our internal belief structure, which is the foundation of our identity and personality. Whenever we create something new, our negative and limiting beliefs will jump up and try to derail us. Doing something new is dangerous to our primitive mind and our our childhood beliefs. It's much safer to keep doing the same things we've always done. That's the level you have to work with in order to melt away the resistance.

There is good news amidst all these revelations: you *have* beliefs, but you *are not* your beliefs. Who you *are* is a unique light shining out in all directions. What's in the way of your light shining are these old programs operating at the subconscious level. Beliefs can be changed and deleted completely. Doing so is not difficult if you have the right tools (and you put in the time to do your inner work). This is a lifelong journey, and the reward are well worth the effort. Life keeps getting sweeter and more beautiful. You get to connect with really wonderful people along the way. Love and wisdom bloom, and new possibilities open in front of you. You get to shine your light and give your gifts to the world.

None of us can do this alone. We need wise guides who have the knowledge and the tools to help us, holding a safe space for our exploration and our excavation project. Then, in the cleared space, you get to decide what you *want* to believe, because those beliefs will bring you the experiences you want, and the life you want.

Clear the way so your divine light can shine.

Dr John Demartini

– Dr John F. Demartini, Human Behavior Specialist, Educator, Business Consultant and Internationally Published Best-selling Author

John Demartini started 1st grade being identified by his teacher as a left-handed learning-disabled dyslexic. She advised his parents that he probably wouldn't come to much and he was placed in remedial class. At 14 years of age, John dropped out of school to follow his dream of surfing in California, and Mexico. He left with the blessing of his parents and a notarised letter in his pocket confirming he was not a runaway. From California at age 15 he then made his way to Hawaii in pursuit of surfing ever larger waves. There at age 17 he nearly died. In recovery, he met a special mentor one evening that changed his life and inspired him to believe he could overcome his learning challenges and someday actually be able to read, write and speak effectively and become linguistically intelligent. That was the evening he dreamed of learning effectively and becoming a teacher who traveled the world. For the last 49+ years, John followed his inspired journey learning to read, write and speak effectively and gradually developing the science of love and appreciation and how to make meaningful dreams come true which he now shares with the world through The Breakthrough Experience – which includes his Demartini Method - a revolutionary new approach to Personal Transformation and many other programs.

"The moment you realize you already have everything you're looking for; the universe gives it to you."
~John Demartini

Your Life Mission

Requiring outside or extrinsic motivation is a symptom of not living your life by your highest value and intrinsic driven mission or calling

Your outer influences, such as your mothers, fathers, preachers, teachers, conventions and traditions can cloud the clarity of your true calling. This is when you find yourself being a cat trying to swim like a fish. Or beating yourself up because you're trying to be somebody you're not, instead of being authentic; that's a symptom that you're not following your true calling.

All symptoms, in every area of your life, offers you feedback; they may be in your physiology, psychology, sociology, or businesses. Your symptoms guide you to authenticity, to the expression of your soul.

True unconditional love (as described in many ancient texts) is about giving yourself permission to live authentically by prioritising and acting upon what is deeply meaningful to you each day and in a way that equitably and sustainably serves others.

When you do something sustainable and receive fair exchange or remuneration for your services, you can do what you love and love what you do daily. This liberates you from the bondage of disempowerment and a quiet life of desperation.

You are here to do something extraordinary! You are not here to play small. The magnificence of who you truly and fully are is far greater than any fantasies you'll ever impose on yourself. You're not here to subordinate to others and to cloud the clarity of your own mission, nor to live in anyone's shadow.

When you put someone on a pedestal, you focus more on their perceived positive traits and ignore their negative ones, and when you put someone in a pit, you focus more on the perceived negative traits and ignore the positive ones. When you judge people by putting them on pedestals or pits instead of putting them in your heart with reflective awareness, then you have deflective awareness and end up with disowned parts. When you do, you are too humble or proud to admit that what you admire or dislike inside them is indeed inside of you.

You split your full consciousness into conscious and unconscious halves. This is not being mindful; it's mindless – you function from your brain's amygdala and react emotionally. Every time you don't balance your equation, by mindfully seeing both sides, you store these imbalanced perceptions in your subconscious mind as wounds or fantasies, which can cause you to react emotionally before you think.

When you neutralize that stored judgment and liberate yourself from this subconscious storage, you are able to transform this your judgment into a more balanced and transcendental awareness. Then you will have the new awareness stored in your superconscious mind, and experience grace and love for what's happened. You will then perceive the issue as an experience on the way, not in the way.

So often, you can hold yourself bound with baggage instead of liberating yourself to get up and fly; to do what you feel you are truly here to do. Anything you can't say thank you for is baggage. Anything you can say thank you for is fuel. Anything you don't love, runs our life until you finally love it.

The Breakthrough Experience and the Demartini Method is designed for clearing that. It's a simple cognitive questioning process to make you aware of what we do not love in our lives, and it gives you a series of questions to answer and hold yourself accountable to so that you can love and appreciate again. When you are able to reflect on both sides of the story, you are able to liberate yourself by loving unconditionally. Once you awaken to the hidden order in your apparent chaos you become liberated and inspired.

The Buddha said, "The desire for that which is unavailable and the desire to avoid that which is unavoidable is the source of human suffering."

Objective Questioning for Truth

When you polarize your mind with subjective bias, you don't see the truth, you don't see the whole, and you become emotionally reactive. You get caught in your judgments and weigh yourself down.

When you ask intuitive and meaningful questions, you lighten yourself up, which liberates you from subjective biases, so you can see the objective truth. When you recognise the hidden order, you are graced by it and realize that everything in your life is there to guide you to your authentic path.

By loving unconditionally, you can have wholeness, wellness, and well-being. The universe is magnificently designed to make sure you grow. If you open your heart and mind to the magnificence of what you are and what's around you, you build momentum towards something extraordinary for the planet.

In The Breakthrough Experience program, I ask you to identify somebody who you admire and think is greater than yourself in some capacity. (That's your illusion because you're being too humble to admit that what you see in them is actually inside you.) I ask you to identify somebody who's done extraordinary things on the planet. I ask you, "What specific traits, actions or inactions do you perceive this individual displaying or demonstrating that you admire most?" Then you have to remember a series of moments when you perceived yourself displaying the same or similar traits, actions, or inactions equally.

I hold you accountable because you would not see such behaviours in others if you cannot recognise them introspectively within yourself. When you realize that these behaviours are hiding in you, but you've been too proud or too humble to admit it, you are often moved to tears of gratitude, when you awaken inside yourself the realisation that they are not missing in you. At the level of the essence of your soul, nothing's missing. At the level of your existent senses things appear to be missing. You are a hero and a villain, a saint and a sinner, virtuous and vicious and all other complementary opposites, because your virtue and vice is different according to your individual values, and they're all just transient illusions of your mind. When you finally realize you have everything, nothing's missing.

Once you fully realize you have everything, you consciously act as if you have and people recognise that within you. There's a wholeness because you value your complete self, and so does the world. You value yourself when you realize nothing's missing.

Traits that Trigger You

* * *

30

Thirty-eight years ago, I went through the Oxford Dictionary and underlined every human behavioural trait that I could find. I found 4,628 individual traits. I wrote in the margin the initials of the most extreme example of someone who displayed that trait to the fullest in my perception. Then I did self-reflection, introspection, and analysis of myself. I perceive myself displaying or demonstrating that particular trait, action, or inaction. I kept doing it until I could own all of the traits 100%, as much as I perceived in them, in the most extreme example that I could perceive of the individual I had initially thought of. When I owned it, there was liberty instead of an emotional trigger.

It is only because of your disowned parts that people push your buttons. The things you are not willing to face in yourself - the hero and the villain side, what you like and dislike. your shadow is not even a shadow, and your light is not even a light because they both have Yin and Yang in them; they both have all. They're just illusions. The very trait you might admire in somebody may eventually aggravate you too.

It took months of work to go through 4,628 traits, but it saved me time from having to react to people. Who am I to judge them? I'm that too. I'm not a nice person; I'm not a mean person - those are just personas. I am an individual with both sides at times.

I'm a whole individual. If you support my values, I can be nice as a pussycat, and if you challenge my values, I can be mean as a tiger. I don't need to get rid of any part of myself. The idea of one-sided moral hypocrisy is the delusion that traps people. The wholeness, the perfection, is the embracing of all of it. When we finally embrace all of that, it doesn't run us because we're not trying to hide it anymore.

I realised that I don't need to get rid of any part of myself to love myself, and I certainly don't need to fix anybody else; they have all the traits too. I learned that if I can love all those traits and see how they all serve, I can appreciate other people for being who they are. We all want to be loved for who we are.

Whatever you think you can repress, you draw it into your life.

Giving other individuals the opportunity or so-called permission to be themselves is liberating. I'd rather encourage people to honor that instead of trying to get rid of half themselves by trying to fit into a box or a fantasy. So, burn the mask.

No matter what you've been through in life, whether you've been supported or challenged, realize that these complementary opposites are synchronously paired. Whenever you experience somebody bullying, challenging, and criticising you, there will also be an over-protector, praiser and supporter. The more you're addicted to the supporter and protector, the more you have to have the critical bully to keep you in authentic equilibrium. If the support and praise get you proud and puffed up, the criticiser brings you back down into authenticity. They always come as a pair. You often become conscious of one side and unconscious of the other but both are entangled and present either in reality or virtual reality.

Complementary Opposites of Perception

Wilhelm Wundt, a psychologist who lived over 100 years ago, talked about simultaneous contrast and sequential contrast. The majority of people live in sequential contrast; they have an event where somebody's nice to them, and then there's another event that somebody is mean to them; they gyrate by external perturbation. Wilhelm Wundt called this sequential contrast. When you're present and more fully conscious of both sides simultaneously, you realize that they are just pairs of opposites keeping you centered and authentic.

When your life is liberated, you realize that it's actually an act of love, because love is a synthesis and synchronicity of these complementary pairs of opposites of perception. You may unwisely call these experiences good or bad when you become caught in a moral construct instead of transcending them by seeing both sides simultaneously. When you do, you liberate yourself from the bondage of the one-sided thinking - seeking and avoiding all the time. When fully whole and present, you don't have to seek and avoid.

The Objective View

Resilience and adaptability come with an objective or neutral view, as opposed to a subjective bias. When you listen to your intuition, you ask the right questions. Your intuition tries to bring you - through a negative feedback loop - into homeostasis and authenticity. If you are aware and listen to it astutely instead of being caught in the impulses of pleasure and the instincts of pain, you are able to see both sides simultaneously and you are able to be grateful.

You are not here to be a victim of your history; you are here to be a master of your destiny. When people come to The Breakthrough Experience, they often want to run their story. I tell them: "Stop. Stop the story. If you want to grow, there's nothing to blame – not even yourself. There's something to gain an understanding of - there's something to find and extract wisdom from - but there's nothing to blame. So, stop the story and focus on priority. You start to see how there are two sides to events, and once the event is liberated and balanced, you don't have a victim story. All you have is thank you, I love you." The story means nothing. Love and thank you is what is liberating.

"Your emotions are feedback mechanisms to let you know you have an incomplete awareness, that's all."

Once you balance your mind, your physiology normalizes and heals, and all of a sudden, you're grateful for life again. All of your emotions are feedback mechanisms to let you know that you haven't seen the whole event yet. You're seeing part of it, and you're reacting to your incomplete awareness. Your emotions serve you in that respect. If you know how to interpret them wisely, they guide you back. All emotions are nothing more than feedback mechanisms to guide you to authenticity.

The Science of Grief

Since 1984, I have been helping people work through their perceptions of loss and the accompanying grief with the Demartini Method, dissolving it. It is an amazing and effective science that is inspiring to observe. You don't have to prolong or wallow in it. It isn't actually assisting your physiology, nor respecting the individual who has passed, because you will not meet anyone that can honestly say that when they die that they want the people they care about to grieve; they want their loved ones to live their lives to the fullest.

Grieving is holding on to an incomplete awareness of that individual instead of actually showing appreciation and love for the whole of them. When you truly love and appreciate them, the grief dissolves and you feel their presence not their loss; your grief's done, you're present with them. You feel their presence, whether they're alive or dead. You feel their presence and their contribution to your life and you are complete and grateful.

I've taken over 4,000 people through the Demartini Method grief process. I did an experiment at Keio University in Tokyo. In the study, we took people with prolonged grief syndromes who had been at least six months to many years in grief and helped them dissolve it. Two hours and 17 minutes was the average time. We followed them up for a month, three months, six months, one year, 18 months - no grief.

There's a methodology that you can now do. Most people don't believe that it's possible, but you can turn grief into a deep love and appreciation of the passing and inspiration once you know how to use this new option.

Depression often comes from comparing one current reality to a fantasy of how life is supposed to be. Holding on to those unrealistic expectations makes it impossible to appreciate reality. If you compare what's real to a fantasy, you'll never appreciate what's real. There's a way of asking questions to neutralize and appreciate reality and break such an illusion. Once people learn how to do that, they don't have to be bogged down in disappointment or depression. They get on with their lives.

Instead, people get lost in blaming, living in moral hypocrisies, assuming a drug is supposed to take care of it, and they never really learn how to use the science of this method through their own mind and body to overcome their blocks and do something more liberated and extraordinary.

The master lives in a world of transformation, not of the illusions of gain and loss. When the fantasy you have about the individual who passed is dissolved and grounded, you feel the individual's true presence and love for them. You close your eyes and feel that you are right there with that individual. You get to say your gratitude and express the love that you were not able to express before. You get to break through the infatuations you previously had - confused as love - and the buried disappoint behaviours that are now relieved and honor their wholeness with a more transcendent love.

Many people say that it's actually guilt they feel and not grief, because they thought the way they interacted with the individual that passed the very last time was not balanced or complete. They didn't get to say thank you. Once it's balanced, they say thank you and express love for them, then the grief dissolves. It's amazing, and it's reproducible science. You don't grieve the loss of a villain; you only grieve the loss of your hero or someone you have admiration or infatuation for. The moment you see more positives than negatives, you fear their loss. The moment you see more negatives than positives, you fear their gain. When you see them balanced, there's no fear of gain or loss; there's only love.

When you allow yourself to master and balance your perception, things or events externally don't run you. Anything you are infatuated with is going to occupy space and time in your mind and run you. Anything you resent can occupy space and time in your mind and run you. You can only be free if you love and appreciate everything. Learning how to ask questions that balance your perception changes your decisions, which changes your actions. If you act from love, you're acting from inspiration, and it's spontaneous, and you don't have to decide out of incomplete perceptions of phobic fear or philic fantasy.

When you look in the mirror and compare yourself to anybody else, you won't appreciate yourself to the fullest. You will either puff yourself up into inauthenticity or beat yourself up into inauthenticity. However, if you look in the mirror without comparing yourself to anybody, only your own daily actions to what's most meaningful to you, and you'll realize the magnificence of who you are. When you do, you'll be grateful for your life, and you'll have so many things to be thankful for. You'll do something incredible that makes a difference. Be an un-borrowed visionary, not a borrowed visionary of conformity; do something of enormity.

I have nothing to hide or regret in my life; I'm grateful. In the journey of your life, anything you can't say thank you for becomes your baggage. If you are not grateful for yourself and your life's journey - you're not seeing the whole; you see illusions. When you look back and really see what it is in its entirety, you'll see that you wouldn't have it any other way. That's a magnificent path. And then you can be grateful for your life, and those who are grateful get more to be grateful for.

The 7 Quality Questions you can ask yourself:
1. What is it I would absolutely love to do or create in life?
2. How would I get handsomely or beautifully paid to do it?
3. What are the highest priority actions I can do today to make it happen?
4. What obstacles might I run into and how do I solve them in advance?
5. What worked and what didn't work today?
6. How can I do it more efficiently and effectively tomorrow?
7. How, no matter what happened, is this helping me fulfil my mission?

Connect at   www.drdemartini.com

Dr Joe Vitale

Dr. Joe Vitale is the globally famous author of numerous bestselling books, from The Attractor Factor to Zero Limits. He's a musician, magician, marketer and worldwide celebrity urging people to go for their dreams. He's the host of "Zero Limits Living" TV show, founder of Miracles Coaching, a star in the hit movie The Secret, and more. See www.MrFire.com

"It's all in your head. You have the power to
make things seem hard or easy or even amusing.
The choice is yours."
~ Seneca

When you follow your mission, life works

I was homeless 40 years ago, and I lived in poverty for ten years. But for the past two decades, I have been living the lifestyle of the rich and famous. You may know me because of my books, my audios, my coaching and mentoring programs, my speeches around the world, or the fact that I was in a bunch of movies, the most famous being *The Secret*, but none of that matters. I have taught myself that the Law of Attraction works, and I have become a teacher and guide.

Yet, despite all my knowledge, in the past two years and at the age of 67, I have endured an excruciating, agonising and expensive divorce, which felt like persecution. During this same period, my father died, my best friend died, and a family member attempted suicide. I formed a new relationship with a woman who fell gravely ill with Lyme disease, and I faced losing her too as I sat by her bedside. On top of all this, the Covid lockdown removed much of my income as a speaker.

Funny, just this morning, I was promoting a song I wrote back in 2012 that goes: "Everybody is going through something." It's such a good reminder—life is full of pitfalls, and you can't just pretend that your problems are not there.

Understanding that you are not alone in your troubles is an important place to start when you feel very low, and this is the first step.

Often, we think that we are alone in our feelings, and it can be a great relief when we discover that we are not alone.

The second step is to focus on what you want to create. Recently, my divorce lawyer comforted me with the words: "Focus on the future." Think about what you want to create for yourself, and concentrate on where you want to go so that you don't get stuck feeling like a victim.

Thirdly, don't be afraid to ask for help! Even as a self-help guru all these years, I found myself reaching out to my therapist again recently. No matter who you are, there are times when one needs to humble oneself and ask for help, because even when one feels isolated and in pain, we are not alone. We are here with billions of others on this planet. And when it comes down to it, life is about relationships. It is in relationships that we are hurt and in relationships that we heal.

When we ask for help or go for therapy, we are given the gift of a safe space to be witnessed as we express our thoughts and emotions. A lot of healing comes from being heard. The best way to heal yourself is to simply have no secrets!

Most of us keep everything inside ourselves, and this can create resentment. It's like stockpiling dynamite. Then something small can trigger an inappropriate reaction, like road rage: someone cuts you off in the traffic, and you go ballistic! That's a classic over-reaction to the situation. Talking about the underlying issues relieves a lot of the psychic energy, and being heard provides relief. Therapists are trained to listen non-judgmentally.

Sometimes it's hard to talk about your feelings; this is usually affected by one's upbringing and cultural heritage. My dad was a marine during World War II; he was a boxer, had too much testosterone, and was very macho. For him, holding it together, not crying, not showing pain was a heroic thing, and I grew up hearing that. So, when I'm hurt and I want to cry, I battle with that internal tug of war that says, *No, don't do that; that's not a manly thing to do.* This kind of thing becomes a form of programming.

However, programming is for machines, and we are not robots. So, to get in touch with our humanity, we need to start feeling our feelings and being honest about them.

It seems to me that most of us who were told not to show emotions, like crying in public, don't even do it in private. We try to lock it down, and that is unhealthy. When we bury a feeling, an emotion, we bury it alive. However, it's still in us, even if we may not consciously pay attention to it.

An over-response is the result of all the bottled emotion that wasn't expressed appropriately when it was occurring. We stuffed it down, we made it hidden, but the unconscious didn't forget it. The unconscious let it go underground.

Over time, when you didn't express the anger or you were upset, you just bit your lip. You didn't cry when you were hurt. All the times you suppress your feelings have built up until that moment when somebody says the wrong thing, and suddenly, you are so triggered, you explode.

This is why we need to express our feelings appropriately, either in the present moment or as close to the moment as we're feeling them. Buried feelings are like dynamite; it only takes a little spark to trigger an explosion. These experiences remind us again that we are human, not machines.

Sometimes we have to look at why we don't want to talk about things. We need to honour how we feel, and there may be feelings of shame that hold us back from speaking about something.

Throughout the movie *Good Will Hunting*, Robin Williams, who plays the therapist in the story, says "It's not your fault" eleven times. There's a powerful message in that. When you realize it's not your fault, that secret story you have been guarding—the trauma, the challenge, the embarrassment, and the shame—dismantles.

When we realize that other people involved were probably unconscious of their behaviour, and we may have been unconscious of our own behaviour, we can let go of blame. We can look within ourselves and heal whatever limiting beliefs might have been there or might still be there. We can heal our self-esteem and self-worth, and then we can begin to reclaim our value.

I love the story of the teacher who held up a five-dollar bill to a group of school children. He asked them, "How many of you want this?" The children all raised their hands. Then the teacher scrunched it up and stamped on it. He unfolded it again and asked who wanted it. They all raised their hands again. He then soiled it some more, held it up and asked again who wanted it. All the kids raised their hands again.

He was teaching them that even if you have been abused and soiled, you still have the same value as before. You are still golden; you are still from the Divine. Your intrinsic value has not changed. The fact that you were badly treated is not your fault, and you are still wanted and valued by the world.

It is so important to understand that the Law of Attraction works on a subconscious level. So, unresolved issues can not only affect one's energy levels and health as they reside in one's body causing stress, but they can become a block in one's energy flow, holding back and preventing one from manifesting the life they want to live.

I was in the movie, *The Secret*. A lot of people have heard about the Law of Attraction because of that movie, but they go to apply it, and they tell me, "Well, it doesn't work for me. I can't attract what I want. I can't manifest my dreams."

What's missing is a deeper understanding of how the Law of Attraction works; it works on the subconscious and unconscious, not only on the conscious level.

Many of us don't even realize how much energy we use to keep our past hurts alive. It doesn't have to be some violent, traumatic war zone kind of hurt. It could be something where somebody said something, and you're hurt because of it; maybe it was a trusted friend or a stranger. But they said something that hurt you, and it got lodged in you.

As you keep the unprocessed emotions at bay, you are using up the energy that is available at this moment to create the life you want. While we attempt to suppress the wound, we use up present-day energy to hold it within ourselves.

This is advanced thinking, and the good news is that as soon as we let go of that hurt, the energy that was being burnt up in holding the pain is now available to us to create the life we want.

For the longest time, especially growing up, I was hurt by people who would say the wrong thing at the wrong time. I carried the hurt and anger, and I didn't realize until somebody pointed out decades later that the only person I was hurting by holding on to that hurt was me!

Those looping thoughts become an energy drain; that ball of anger in me never touched the other person, never hurt them, never alerted them, never got near them. Instead, it was burning me up; it was killing me. When I realised that this wasn't working the way I thought it was working, it became clear that I needed to let go of that. I began by bringing some adult awareness and spiritual insight to it. And when it left me, I became not only free, but instead of the energy being used up in a self-destructive way, it started to get used in a self-directed creative way!

My philosophy is that when we follow our mission, life works. When we deny our mission or pretend we don't have a mission or spend so much time focused on past hurts that we don't live our mission, then life kind of limps along. Life has rocky roads for all of us. I think that's part of our journey here on Earth as a people; we are here to awaken to our own personal mission, whatever that happens to be; big or small, it doesn't matter. Follow the light, follow the juice, the passion in your life to express your particular life mission.

Sometimes, it's not that easy to just let go of something terrible that happened to you. There are other ways to transform the energy of the pain you endured.

Debbie Ford, the author of books like *The Dark Side of the Light Chasers* and *Spiritual Divorce*, was an enlightened teacher I knew and loved. I remember her advising a woman who was angry about things in history regarding women's rights. Debbie's guidance to her was, "Well, if you want to hold on to your anger, you can use it, and you can use it to create something that makes a difference."

She was saying let's move it in a new direction and use the high voltage energy of anger to repair whatever caused you to be angry in the first place.

The philosophy of the stoics Marcus Aurelius, Epictetus, Seneca have helped me get through the past two years. The Stoics point out that the challenges you're going through right now are developing a latent strength within you that wouldn't develop without the challenge. Now, this is an important concept. I don't want to feel like a victim; I want to be in power. So, when things got rough recently and I was having a hard time, it helped to realize that this was an opportunity to develop the parts of me that were on the weak side, the undeveloped side, the latent side.

For example, Hercules would never have been Hercules if he didn't have things to struggle with. If he had had an easy life, eating fast food and ice cream every day and then going to sleep, we'd never have heard of his character! It's only because Hercules had to go and fight the challenges in front of him that we know of him; his challenges built his muscles and created what a superhero is to a lot of people.

Clearing the energy of the past hurts subconsciously, and manifesting the life you want to live requires regular energy clearing and prayer as a spiritual practice. My book *Zero Limits* is about the Ho'oponopono method. This is a mantra made famous by a doctor in Hawaii who used it in a mental hospital for dangerous mentally ill criminals. After months of just praying and utilising this method, the in-patients recovered, even though he didn't work with them directly. I heard the story and tracked the founder down. His name is Dr Hew Len, and we co-authored this book.

Dr Hew Len took the job at the mental hospital; his method was observing what he considered a problem inside himself as a prayer to the Divine. He repeated four phrases: *I love you, I'm sorry, please forgive me, thank you.* In any order, he didn't say them out loud, nor did he say them to the patients. He spoke them only silently inside of himself as he was feeling whatever he was feeling, and as a way of communication with the Creator.

Dr Hew Len explained that he shifted his perception deeply by doing this, which changed the actual scenario. He was working on his own perception of mentally ill criminals. This is a crucial distinction because the Ho'oponopono works on your perceptions of your life, your problems, relationships, the traumas you went through. It clears your perceptions of the experience. Everything is inside of you! When you think about it, all the things you perceive as problems aren't out there; your perceptions are from within you. They're triggered by something you believe to be out there, but the trigger is in you. So, it's essential to bring it back home.

Consider something that's bothering you right now: it may be another person, an experience you've gone through, a trauma, a challenge. Whatever the problem is, focus on it for a moment; allow it just to come inside of you. Everything that you were thinking about, feeling, considering is all in you. As you're feeling it, imagine that you're calling up God; whatever your version of God is—we all have different words for it. It can be your higher self, "all that is," or your preferred name, and you're saying, "Whatever is going on in me, take care of it, remove it, clean it, clear it." The request is those four phrases: *I love you, I am sorry, please forgive me, thank you.* You can say them in any order.

I love you, I'm sorry, please forgive me, thank you. It's a kind of shorthand for a lot more.

When you're saying things like "please forgive me", you're not saying you're at fault, you're not saying you're wrong, you're not saying you need to be punished. You're saying, "Please forgive me, because I am unaware of my own belief systems and programming. I don't know what's in my subconscious or unconscious mind; I'm sorry for being unconscious."

The example I use is, when you go to a crowded place and you accidentally bump into somebody, don't you naturally turn and say "I'm sorry"? And why? You said you were sorry because you didn't see them there. Why didn't you see them there? Because you were unconscious, you were focused on something else. So, when you say "I'm sorry" and "Please forgive me", you're basically saying, "I wasn't aware of my subconscious beliefs. I'm sorry; please forgive me for that."

"Thank you" is a statement of gratitude, which is one of the most beautiful things any of us can do at any time. Thank you for healing me, clearing me, and cleaning me of these particular beliefs, whatever they may be; you don't need to know what the beliefs are. Thank you for erasing them.

I think that if we just walked around saying "I love you" inside of ourselves, our lives would change forever! We don't have to say it to the other person, just inside our heads. If we say "I love you; I love you, I love you, I love you" as we go about our day, our face, our energy, our vibrations, everything will transform. In the context of the Ho'oponopono prayer, you are saying to the Divine, "I love you for my life. I love you for my process. I love you for taking care of me, I love you for always being with me."

All of these four phrases have layers of meaning, but all you have to do is notice what's going on, whatever you're upset about. Even if it looks like it's out there, it's not about anything out there; that's the mirage. The trigger is in here, and as you feel the trigger, you don't even have to know all about it. This is not psychotherapy. You don't need to go and analyse and find beliefs. The Ho'oponopono takes care of transforming them.

After doing this for 15 years, it becomes automatic for me; I'm here, doing my best to be present, not allowing any memories, influence, preconceived ideas, prejudices, judgments, or anything to come in outside of the Divine at this moment. At the same time, the mantra keeps playing at the back of my mind. *I love you, I am sorry, please forgive me, thank you.*

I invite you to dive deeper into the practice of Ho'oponopono. There's lots of information on the internet. I've authored three books on it. *Zero Limits* was the first one, shaking the world awake. Ten years later, I wrote *At Zero*. The third book, which came out recently, is called *The Fifth Phrase*. That's the more advanced version.

And the teachings go deeper.
Ao Akua!
Joe Vitale

Tracey Gazel

Tracey Gazel is an Energy Expert and Soul Purpose Coach for Empaths. Her mission is to help all empaths realize how gifted and powerful they truly are. She is the Founder of Rising Higher Consulting, a coaching agency that helps empaths around the world use their empathic gifts to heal themselves and activate their purpose.
www.traceygazel.com

"Your trauma is a stepping stone helping you step into your soul purpose"
~ Tracey Gazel

Activate Your Purpose

Everything changed the day my Dad passed away. I never imagined the Universe would take me on such a wild ride to arrive at my soul's life purpose that would help you remember yours.

The day before Dad's passing, my husband and I were walking our dog in our neighbourhood. I felt broken inside as if my body was about to fall apart at the seams. Dad had been terminally ill and was in the hospice and after the long months of his debilitation, I needed to clear my head.

It was then I noticed a sign in a shop window that read 'Angel Card Readings Inside'. I had never had a card reading before as it was not something I believed in, however, something told me that I needed to go inside.

My skepticism was evident in my voice as I turned to my husband and said, "I'm going inside to ask about the angel card reading but I'm only going to pay $10". I entered and asked the woman at the counter how much an Angel Card Reading would cost. She looked me up and down and said, "For you, $10". It became apparent to me that I had to say yes! She then flipped over one card, looked at me, and said, "The Universe is waiting for you to tell it what you want".

Chills ran over my entire body. My grief until now had prevented me from asking what was at the core of my being. I wanted to know that my Dad was going to be free of his pain and suffering after he died. I needed to know that his soul wouldn't simply extinguish along with his dying body.

The next morning, friends and family gathered at the Hospice to say their last goodbyes. Dad lay heavily sedated in the hospital bed, his body contorted in an awkward position from the pain he had to endure. He looked nothing like the Dad I remembered as a small child. The Dad who every night would be there to read me stories and spend special moments together.

At that moment I was ready to ask the Universe for what I wanted. I looked at my Dad, hoping he could hear me as he lay there unresponsive. His breathing was laboured, and it rattled in his chest, his skin was pale and paper-thin. I asked for a miracle. "Dad, I know you need to go. I can't fix you no matter what I try. When your body dies, can you stay with me for a little while? I don't know if this is possible but I'm not ready to let you go." I felt like I was five years old again, begging him to not stop reading the story to me, even though I was now in my twenties.

His eyes were closed, but he started to sob. He could hear me. Together we held each other until a friend came in to soothe us. That evening as we were preparing to leave, he took a turn for the worse and the nurse advised, "He's close to passing away and he doesn't want to be alone. Are you able to stay?"
Together with my Mom, we held his hands and comforted him, telling him that we would be okay when he left. We told him not to worry about us. We told him that we would be safe and that we would take care of each other. As his breathing slowed, I saw my Dad, my hero, begin to slip away and forever leave his physical form. It wasn't peaceful. It wasn't like the stories we read where someone quietly passes away, lying on their back with their hands comfortably crossed over their chest. It was frightening to watch, and it was made worse seeing him scared and trying to fight it. He didn't want to die. Within a few minutes, he was gone. All that was left of him was his human body lying there still, and so obviously vacant. I couldn't breathe. I began hyperventilating as I tried to catch my breath. It was as if all the oxygen in the room had left with him.

That night I was beyond exhausted but also too tired to sleep. I poured myself a whisky and when I began to feel like I was melting into my couch; I knew it was time to go to bed. When I finally drifted off to sleep, I had a dream that was like no other dream I had experienced before. I saw my Dad standing in front of me. He was wearing his signature outfit of jeans and a plain white T-shirt, and he was back to his healthy self. He said to me, "Tracey, I need you to know that I'm OK". And then he showed me the infinity sign. The message was clear to me. We, our souls, are infinite. Death is not final and the 'real' us never really dies. And then he was gone.

A few days later I took a mountain bike ride with my husband. After spending two years watching my Dad die from a terminal illness, I thought I would feel relieved when he finally passed. All I felt however was the immense weight of grief wrapping around my body like a heavy cloak. On the downward descent of the trail, something caught the corner of my eye. A male deer with large antlers was standing still in the shadows of the forest. I brought my bike to a stop, and I made eye contact with him. I reveled in the moment and then continued on. As I peddled up to speed on the downward descent, I heard my Dad's voice speaking to me as clear as day. He was laughing, and it sounded like he was having a lot of fun, making the sounds he used to when he would ride the rollercoaster. As I traveled over the bumps and turns, I heard him say "Woo Hoo! Tracey, I can see why you like mountain biking; this is so much fun!"

My mind started racing almost as fast as my bike. There must be something wrong with me. Why was I hearing voices? While studying for my psychology degree I had learned that if anyone says they are hearing voices, it is possible they are delusional and they must be sent to the hospital's psychiatric ward right away. I felt fear tingle through my mind; was I having a psychotic break? Could it be possible that I had asked my Dad to stay with me, and he did. Could it be possible that I asked for a miracle, and I had received it. As I reached the end of the trail, my husband was waiting for me. I was relieved it was a sunny day and that my sunglasses were able to hide my tears of disbelief. My fear prevented me from sharing the experience with my husband. It became my secret from everyone. I decided I needed to fix myself.

The following day, I set about using my meditation training to see if it would help me to understand what was happening. I closed my eyes and settled my energy with my breath. I noticed my aura surrounding my body like a curtain. Then I noticed a density of energy standing beside me. And, as I asked it questions, I heard my dad's voice reply. My mind once again filled with fear, doubt, and skepticism, yet it felt real when I tuned into my intuition and my gut which came with a knowing from deep within my bones.
Eventually, I contacted the only person I knew who would possibly understand. My meditation teacher, Duncan, responded immediately. After expressing his condolences, he shared that he was happy I was receiving visitations. He also said, "What a divine coincidence, next week I am starting a new class about how to communicate with beings out of the body. Would you like to join us?" I had to say yes! This training was another signpost from the Universe that I was headed in

the right direction.

The teachings were easy for me, and I learned how to connect with the presence of my father, as well as other divine souls not residing in a body. Already so sensitive to energy, this was just another way to direct my focus.

It was just a matter of weeks, however, when my mind started to chatter again. Is this really all in my head? What if I really do have a mental health disorder? Who do I think I am to receive a miracle?

I decided I would ask for a sign. I pleaded out loud, "If this is really true and I'm able to connect to my Dad, show me some kind of sign." Almost immediately, I was guided to reach into the pocket of the jeans I was wearing, and I pulled out a circular white sticker that had the number 8 on it. I had never seen it before. I stared in disbelief as I turned it on its side and the 8 became the infinity sign from my dream. I had asked for a sign and the Universe had responded.

Connecting with my Dad each morning became part of my daily meditation practice. I would check-in and ask him if there was anything I needed to know for the day. Most days he would remind me to take care of myself and to love myself. He was always very cheerful and upbeat, and it was heartwarming to hear him talk like he used to before he was sick. He would tell me that he missed eating food but other than that he was doing well. It was an everyday miracle that became commonplace. As I moved beyond fear and doubt and into a space of acceptance, I began to feel safe in sharing it with others. Although they couldn't quite understand how it was possible, they were all very supportive of me.

I came to learn that we are all souls living in a temporary body and there is no true 'death'. And, due to the temporary nature of this lifetime, I came here with a unique intention, a soul purpose, that I signed up to experience.

I now know that this is a benevolent universe that is available to all of us just beyond the tangible reality of everyday life. It's possible to ask for a miracle and to receive one, and it's possible to live a miraculous life.

The trauma of my father's death is not something that I would choose to relive but I am forever grateful for who I became as a result. I stepped into the empowered, vibrant, and thriving version of myself that is aligned with my soul. My Dad's death was the rebirth of who I truly am, and it ignited the purpose I came into this lifetime to fulfil. This is how I now want to help you.

I want to make it easier for you to go from pain to purpose. To view your trauma as a gift that invites you to step into your fullness and to activate the soul purpose that you've been searching for your whole life.

Prior to my dad's passing, I had resigned myself to staying in a corporate job that I wasn't passionate about. I had accepted that I would never fulfil my dreams of helping others heal themselves or write a book. Only once I realised that our souls are infinite and this lifetime is but a moment on our soul journey, I choose to live without fear. I was ready to step into my power. I resigned from my corporate job, and I began working as a coach helping those, who are empaths and sensitives, learn how to heal themselves and to align with their soul so that they too can activate their purpose.

When I stopped hiding who I really was, my journey began to speed up and all the pieces began to fall into place. I started to work in partnership with the universe rather than continuing to question it. I felt comfortable coming out of the spiritual closet and sharing my true colors with my family and friends, regardless of their beliefs. I chose to accept that miracles are commonplace.

There's a reason you're reading this chapter. The Universe is sending **you** an invitation to align with your soul and activate your purpose. I'm here to share with you a shortcut to find your purpose that I have used to help hundreds of clients across six different countries.

The trauma that you've been forced to endure holds the keys to unlocking your purpose.

There is purpose in your pain. Your trauma provides an opportunity to make the world a better place based on what you've experienced. Perhaps you want to help others who are going through a similar experience that you have now healed from? Or maybe you're passionate about influencing policy change at the government level to prevent what happened to you from happening to others? What you choose to create in the world based on your trauma is unique to you.

There are many examples from others who have, too, found purpose in their pain. Mothers Against Drunk Driving (MADD) was created by Candace Lightner whose 13-year-old daughter was killed by a drunk driver. Cari was struck as a pedestrian by a three-time repeat offender who was just released from jail two days prior due to a DUI. Cari became the first face of drunk driving victims and her mother worked tirelessly to change drunk driving laws. She turned her pain into her purpose by creating an organisation that is still thriving today working to end drunk and drugged driving.

Oprah Winfrey lived in poverty and suffered abuse for years. As her mother worked long hours as a maid, Oprah was neglected. At nine years old, she was left in the care of her 19-year-old cousin who raped her. At 14, she became pregnant (the baby died shortly after birth) and she moved in with her father in Tennessee. Her father encouraged her to get an education which is where Oprah found her passion for journalism, drama, and public speaking. She became the highest-rated talk show host in history where she built a career interviewing other people and sharing their stories. Because of her own experience with trauma, she is a gifted interviewer who sees the humanity in all people.

Malala Yousafzai was born in Pakistan. At the age of 11, she was vocal in public about how girls should have the right to learn and have an education as boys do. In 2012 on her way home from school, a masked gunman from the Taliban boarded her school bus and asked for Malala. When he found her, he shot her in the head, yet she survived the ordeal after months of surgeries and rehabilitation. Rather than staying quiet, Malala continued her fight, speaking publicly in the UK until every girl had the right to go to school. She received the Nobel Peace Prize in 2014.

What if I told you there was no shame in experiencing trauma? And that your trauma provides inspiration to contribute positively to the world, unlocking your Soul's purpose?

I invite you to take a few minutes to complete my *Purpose Activator Exercise*. Find your favorite journal, curl up in your favorite chair, and do anything else that helps you to relax and go within.

Start by taking five deep breaths through your nose and into your belly. With every exhale, set the intention for your body to relax more. Then turn your focus to your heart space, located in the center of your chest, just behind the breastbone.

From your heart space, I invite you to reflect on the following three questions. Write in your journal all responses that arise. As you write, allow more information to come through your heart and be expressed. Keep writing until your heart is quiet and your responses feel complete. Do your best to not overthink it. Allow the information to flow from your heart rather than from your thinking mind.

1. Who were you as a person before your trauma happened to you?
2. Who did you become as a result?
3. What are three lessons you learned because of your trauma?

Now let's go one step deeper.

1. If you could share one lesson from Question #3 with others, knowing that it would contribute positively to the world, which lesson would it be? Take a few minutes to write your reflections.

Once your answer feels complete, I invite you to put your journal down. Later in the day, revisit your journal and read through what you wrote. Take some time to process the information that your heart center has shared with you.

Your response to Question #3 is the work that you signed up to experience during this lifetime so that your Soul can continue to grow and expand.

Your response to Question #4 is part of your Soul purpose. Is there one small action step that you can take today towards accomplishing this goal?

You are so much bigger than your trauma. Your trauma is a stepping stone helping you step into your highest Soul purpose.

Get my free quiz to discover Your Soul Purpose www.soulpurposequiz.net

Nunaisi Ma

— Nunaisi Ma is a Bestselling Author, Transformational Leader, and founder of *The Rise Movement*. Nunaisi, certified in dozens of healing modalities is helping people transform their life story, unlock their divine genius and live their Soul mission

In 2012, Nunaisi let go of her successful business to align with her Soul mission. Together with her partner and three young children, she traveled the world for four years and lived in the most profound spiritual hubs on Earth. On this journey, Nunaisi has worked with world- recognised therapists, shamans, healers and medicine people.

"It is in processing your most challenging life events where you find the keys to unlock your inner doors of genius"
~Nunaisi Ma

The Key to Upgrade Your Life

"Stop! I have a headache!" she screams and for a moment I stop fighting her and let loose my grip on her stripy pink dress. "Maybe mama is swallowing all these pills *because* she has a headache," I think briefly.

My dad has warned me that I need to look out for her. Lately, they had had violent fights. Mama wants to get out of the marriage and go into the arms of her new lover. "She is threatening to commit suicide," he tells me.

So, I carry on fighting her with all my six-year-old strength... but she still swallows most of the pills.

Picking up my screaming baby brother from the floor, she thrusts him at me and looks me in the eye, "Look after him" and goes to lie down on her bed.

I run outside, knocking on all the neighbours' doors, begging them for help.

Someone calls an ambulance. In the hospital, she has her stomach pumped. It saves her life.

A month later, she tries to kill herself again, rolling her car off a cliff. Grace saves her this time.

Life was never the same for me. I take on the role of being the responsible adult to ensure my mother wanted to live and, in this process, I lost my childhood. I considered that if her lover is the only reason she wants to live, then I should help her get together with him. Every day, I walk to his office and wait there patiently until he writes a note for her so I could bring it home to Mom and make her happy. Soon after, we move into his family's home, together with his three children and crippled wife. Life was chaotic.

Four years later, just after the birth of my sister, when I finally have the courage to offload the heavy secret I am carrying and which has been infecting my being, my mother betrays me. She refuses to believe her boyfriend has been sexually molesting me daily. Instead, she bails him out of jail, telling the judge that I am a liar.

That same day, with none of my belongings, I move to live with my father and his new girlfriend, whom I have only met once. She makes it clear from day one; I am not wanted in her home. She is mean and abusive. The streets became my playground, but they also expose me to the perverts. I have seen too much darkness. I feel broken, not good enough, not worthy, and wrapped in a blanket of shame. In my mid-twenties, I am a mess and am saved just in time from a drug overdose.

Lying on the bathroom floor in my boyfriend's house, I see how I am falling into self-destruction and sabotage. I am tired of feeling sick and tired. It is my wake-up call.

That day, I made a conscious decision to be the hero of my life and not the victim of my story. It was there, when the wise part of my being demanded it, that my redemption began.

In search of Me

As I embarked on my healing journey, I turned over every stone on the path, read every book on the topic, did countless therapies, and traveled the extra mile, far and wide, to look for the building blocks of transformation. I dedicated myself to winning this life over. I was on a quest to feel comfortable in my own skin and to find the meaning of life.

I met outstanding teachers and worked with world-acclaimed therapists, medicine people, and shamans. It was like peeling the layers of an onion; one layer at a time, until all that is left, is an empty space. This is where I met the divine within me.

My healing journey was not a walk in the park. I will not sugar-coat it. Only after feeling the dark depths of my emotional pain, only after many tears had been shed, did I learn to embrace all of me and free myself from my story and from the bondage of my pain. I have dropped the false beliefs that I had about myself. I have also broken the shackles of my lineage as a third generational Holocaust survivor.

The path that I had to pioneer in healing myself allowed me to unlock the mechanics of healing, which is the return to wholeness. This alchemical process, available to all of us, has the potential to turn any wound into a source of power and any pain into purpose.

It is as if I had a contract with the divine before incarnating here on Earth, that I had to go through the training and initiations of a very dysfunctional childhood so that I could experience the journey of healing and then teach this process to others.

Fast forward, almost thirty years later...

I am a proud Mama of three truly incredible, switched-on children. Two of them are already young adults making a positive impact on the world.

I am a bestselling author, transformational leader, and the founder of *The Rise Movement*, which aims to awaken people to their divine nature. My mission is to help you transform your life story and unlock your divine potential so that you too can share your wisdom and impact the world, however you choose to. I have helped thousands of people transform trauma, turn their pain into power and purpose, and rise to their highest selves through my summits, books, online courses, retreats, and personal mentoring.

Whether you had an idyllic childhood, an extremely challenging one, or anything in between, I can tell you this: we've all experienced childhood wounds. You might look back and wish that you had had more love, attention, affection, support, playful adults, protection, sense of belonging, security, resources, guidance, freedom, acceptance, encouragement, acknowledgment, or anything else. No one's childhood was perfect—and for many people, it was harrowing.

Know this, no matter how old you currently are, the child you once were, is still living within you and will be there forever. Your inner child is the truest, most authentic, and innocent core of your being. This essence transcends the artificial confines of your grown self.

Suppose as a child, you grew up in a loving, supportive, and safe environment. In that case, you would then mature into healthy adulthood, naturally full of vitality and passion for life. If as a child, you experienced trauma, wounding, abuse, rejection, unmet needs, lack of acceptance, judgment, criticism, comparison, excessive stress, etc., you might be still struggling to fully mature into adulthood, no matter what your actual age. You might be stuck at a "certain age," subconsciously living life and operating from childlike reactions.

All your childhood memories are alive in your subconscious mind and take residence in the cells of your body, too. These continue to live and interact with your present, influencing how you make choices, respond to challenges, and live your life. You might manage some aspects of your life well while struggling in other areas.

As children, we all developed unconscious beliefs about how we "must" be and what we "must" do to be loved and accepted in our families and society. Our experiences and relational dynamics reinforced these beliefs and formed our own internal script for how our life "should" be. These beliefs often carry into adulthood — in which case they operate in the subconscious mind as the driving force of all our thoughts, feelings, moods, behaviours, actions, triggers, and current relationships. Therefore, it is essential to discover our own script, which is made of all those beliefs about our lives that we keep repeating and recreating. It takes a conscious decision to end the cycle of playing out the same unexamined script and drama repeatedly.

It is natural for children to desire acceptance by the family and the tribe. If a child receives direct or even indirect messages that being oneself is not good enough to get its needs met, if the child's true self is rejected, it must develop a false self, which will result in an inner split between the child's true nature and the personality the child adopts in order to be loved. This false self is made of all the beliefs the child learned, the messages it received, and the role modeling it had. Aspects of the authentic self are then abandoned, causing fragmentation.

Your inner child unconsciously recreates an environment like the one you experienced in childhood by projecting the roles of primary relationships, such as mother, father, and siblings, onto other current relationships. For example, a child's unmet need to be seen by the father will be recreated into an authority figure, such as a partner, teacher, or boss, and be projected onto him. A child who is hurt by excessive criticism from its parents will attract criticism and will scan faces, voices, behaviours, and gestures looking for and therefore finding signs of criticism in the environment while overriding signs of love and support.

Ignoring your inner child does not make it go away; it will keep begging for your attention.

Often when you feel out of control in your behavior or reaction to a situation, it is your inner child acting up. Your inner child might still hold on to all those beliefs you learned as a child—the part of you that accepted when an adult told you that "you can't sing" or a teacher told you how "nothing will come of you." This is the part of you that learned to sweep things under the carpet, behave a certain way, hide, repress emotions, and wear a social mask to be accepted. Your inner child is the Self before you learned to wear masks, change your personality, and present a false self to the world to fit into your family and your culture.

If your inner child is neglected, it will wither away in the deep and dark tomb of your psyche. The longer you bury this primal force within you, the more its energy gets transmuted into the shadows, which then results in you acting out the dark side of your wounded inner child in a messy, dramatic, or destructive way.

You might only have a vague sense of yourself if you were taught as a child to prioritise others' happiness, comfort, and expectations above your own for you to be loved and accepted. If you were moulded to fit a certain religion, tradition, or dogma, you might have renounced your own heart's desires, given up on your dreams, or did things that were not aligned with your true self. You might have adopted the habit of changing your personality depending on who you interact with. While it served as a survival mechanism in your early life to modify your character based on who you were around and who you needed to please, as an adult, you may be unsure of your true identity.

The goal of the inner child's work is to heal those wounds and get back in touch with your authentic self—before the trauma and the harmful experiences—so that you can reconnect with the innocent joy and excitement you experienced as a child, which is your birthright.

Your childhood shaped your life and who you are today. It is the software you download, and which operates you at the backend. Like all software, you can upgrade it to manifest your dream life.

So, watch your inner dialogue. Which voices do you repeat from the past when you talk to yourself?

Are you your biggest supporter and cheerleader, or do you often criticise and put yourself down?
If you would speak to your best friend the way you speak to yourself, will she remain your best friend?
If your answer is "probably not," do this:
Start paying attention to the way you speak to yourself moment to moment. Everything begins with shining the light of your awareness inwardly onto your inner landscape.
If you find yourself being negative, pause.
Place your hand on your heart, take a deep breath and repeat an affirmation, such as

- I am enough

- I do my best

- I am worthy of love

- I am allowed to make mistakes

- I am a perfect imperfection

(I have beautifully made affirmations for you to print on my website www.nunaisi.com/freeresources)

Remember to be kind and gentle with yourself, as if you are treating a young child. This simple action, when repeated as often as required, will rewire your brain to create new neurological pathways. It is through re-parenting your inner child with radical self-acceptance, unconditional love, compassion, and care that you will heal your inner child and upgrade your life. You (and only you) have the power to shift your life and reclaim your sovereign empowerment.
Every child, without exception, has talents, a unique set of traits, skills, and innate wisdom to add to the collective mix of humanity and enrich the world. Sometimes your gifts are second nature to you, so much so that you do not perceive them as gifts,

and you might overlook them. Other times, these talents are hidden as the "golden shadow," named by the psychiatrist Carl Jung, and refers to your submerged creative potential and greatness. You can discover your "golden shadow" in what you were immersed as a child or your current admiration of other people. The bright qualities that you admire (or are jealous of) in others represent the disowned aspects of your unlimited creative potential. Often, these talents are hidden from the world out of a fear of being powerful and successful. Many people, especially women, shrink themselves and play small because they are afraid of being rejected, judged, or criticised, or they are still carrying (like most of us do) ancestral anxiety of prosecution. When you dare to share your golden shadow, this divine aspect of yourself, you become more integrated. You unlock your divine power and can shine your light on the world.

Life is happening for you, not to you. Life stretches and expands with you, and it is out of your comfort zone that you grow the most. It is through the challenges that you meet the depth and the fullness of your being. It is through diving into your darkness that you can then soar to the heights of your soul. There is nothing you need to do to access your divine potential. It is already within you. It is your divine inner child. All you need is to undo what stands in your way to realize it. To drop the mental constructs which you adopted growing up, the limiting beliefs, the conditioning of the wounds and traumas, and the masks you wore to feel loved. All these clouds your clarity of vision. With practice, you see that your wounded child is not only you but may represent several generations. Your parents may have suffered throughout their lives. It is possible that your parents were not able to look after their inner wounded children themselves. When you embrace the wounded child in you, you are embracing all the wounded children of your past generations, too. The healing is not for yourself alone; it is also for countless generations of your ancestors and the generations to come after you.

We all share the same purpose in life... to actualize our divine nature, access our God-given potential, and share our gifts and life lessons with others. We all have unique gifts to share with the world. No one is exempt. How we choose to express our gifts in the world is up to us. We have our own choice and free will. There are infinite ways to do so, and there is no right or wrong. You can share your gifts in any manner of your choosing, be it at home, in the community, or in the marketplace.

I invite you to cultivate radical acceptance of the journey you have walked so far. Know that you are already divine and so loved by many, especially by all the angels that watch over you. So BE the love that you are, your voice matters!

    I have many free transformational tools to assist you in your transformation to become empowered, such as Healing the Inner Child Meditation, Busting Limiting Beliefs workbook, Healing the Mother Wound, transformational summits, and much more.

Visit my website: www.nunaisi.com/freeresources

Lori Montry

Lori is a trauma-informed eating psychology coach who passionately works with women to release them from binge eating, overeating, emotional eating, and chronic dieting. By focusing on the role of the nervous system and the underlying reasons why we struggle with food, Lori empowers her clients to make the choices that allow them to reach their health and weight loss goals. She believes every woman can be FREE! https://www.freedombynuuaria.com.

*"Owning our story and loving ourselves through that process is
the bravest thing that we'll ever do."*
~ Brene Brown

Trading Places

"I'm almost done." These were the only words I remember him
grunting at me as he penetrated my tiny body that was frozen in pain
and confusion. His laboured breathing and the crinkled look on his face
terrified me. A grease-stained hand covered my mouth to keep me from
calling out. He smelled of the garage and it made me feel nauseous. I
was 4 years old and long before I knew what sex was or even how
boys' bodies were different from my own, my innocence was destroyed
by my teenage half-brother.

When he finished, he left me bewildered on the floor of my
bedroom next to my Barbie dolls and board books. The last thing he
said to me was, "This is your fault. If you tell anyone, you'll get in big
trouble. Do you understand me?" I lay there mute, not understanding.
A few minutes later, his loud, brash laugh filled the hallway as he
shared a joke with one of my brothers. It jolted me. I pulled up my
princess panties from around my ankles. It was hard to move from the
throbbing pain between my legs. The rest of me, however, was
completely numb.

This was to be the first of many violations. I lived in constant
terror. Despite my efforts to hide, he always managed to find me. On
one of the first nice days of Spring, his shadow blocked the sunlight
that had been streaming into my outdoor playhouse. My heart fell into
my stomach as I watched him crouch low and enter my special place
where I was making pretend pies and cakes out of mud.

He left my miniature play apron tied around my waist as he helped
himself to my body which had become his plaything like the pots and
pans in my play kitchen. Although I had five older siblings, I was very
much on my own. Everyone had their own lives and activities which
certainly did not include a little girl who was always, 'getting in the
way'. This once playful ally, who had stood up for me against teasing
from my other siblings, had become a hated monster whom I feared.
His laughter no longer brought me joy. It brought me fury. I hated that
I hated him, but I did. I wanted him to disappear, so I never had to see

his stupid expressions, feel his breath on my face, or smell his clothes that always carried the smell of garage grease and dirt.

Each time he violated me, I learned to disassociate more. I began to feel numb not only in those moments of pain and powerlessness but in every other moment as well. I become extremely quiet. I no longer found joy in the normal activities of a child's life. New experiences like starting school were more than my nervous system could handle. I would go to the bathroom and cry until my teacher told me she would call my mother if I didn't come out and finish the sponge painting the rest of the class was working on. I felt terrified at every new experience. I felt overwhelmed by my very existence. I felt certain the next moment would swallow me whole.

Eventually, he moved out of the house. While I was happy to see him go, my carefree childhood did not return.

When I think back to that time, I've wondered why I didn't immediately run into the arms of a loving person or parent and share my terrible secret?

Yes, I was afraid of getting in trouble, but I also didn't feel that I had anyone to turn to. I couldn't burden my mother. I was too afraid of the rage that so often overtook her as she screamed, "I wish I'd never had any goddamn kids." In her eyes, I was another mouth to feed, another butt to wipe. Instead, I kept my shame and despair locked away in my heart. But they didn't go away; they grew like a sprawling root system that affected every aspect of my being.

I survived by becoming frozen inside. I cut off from my body. I don't know when I got my first period or what it was like to experience adolescence. I was numb. I had no friends and felt disconnected from everyone around me. In my mind, no one could be trusted.

It was painful to see my reflection in the mirror and when someone looked at me, I was afraid they would see my ugly secret. I was a monster. Why else would people do bad things to my body? Why else would I be such a burden to my mother?

Tormented by fear, shame, bewilderment, and growing anxiety, I felt desperate for some sort of escape and comfort. I found it in the refrigerator. No one noticed my frequent trips back and forth from the kitchen to my bedroom. Cheese and crackers, chips and dip, Twinkies, and Ding Dongs were plentiful at my house, and they became my trusted companions.

At five years old, all my extra food appeared on my growing belly and thighs. I didn't notice but my mother did. My expanding body triggered her. "You don't want to grow up like me. Being fat is no fun," she would say. I couldn't fit into the small-size clothes she bought me as a means to motivate me to lose weight. Feeling incredibly embarrassed at my body, I tried to pay attention as the doctor explained why I should lose weight and the foods that were 'allowed'. As I listened to the doctor's lecture, I plainly heard, "You must lose weight. You are fat and disgusting. You are not worthy of love and no one will ever like you until you lose weight." I know those words were not spoken but my six-year-old mind heard them as clear as day.

The doctor's words were in fact welcome to me. There was something I could do to become acceptable. If I could lose weight and become thin, people would love me and stop doing bad things to me. I was oddly relieved and optimistic about the new life I assumed I would soon have.

The problem with my plan was that I had no idea how to diet. My 'just don't eat' approach ended up backfiring on me. "All I've had to eat today was an apple," I remember telling Mom once. "Keep it up and you will lose all your weight soon," was her response. My growing body was not as enthusiastic, however. The restrictions would become too much and at some point, I would break down and when I did, I ate until I couldn't eat another bite. It didn't matter what was in the house during those times; my body just wanted calories. I had triggered a survival mechanism left over from the time when we were hunters and gatherers. Periods of restriction triggered my biological drive to eat as much as possible the next time food was available.

After eating until my stomach felt like it would explode, the panic would set in. "What have I done? Why did I do that again?" I'll never lose these pounds. I'm such a loser. God, I hate myself."

The kids at school solidified my status daily. Riding the school bus brought such anxiety and torment that I would feel sick to my stomach as soon as I saw its flashing lights approaching. I once wore my hair in a high bun which drew further cruelty from the boys. "You look like a pig with a fountain on your head." I sunk into the first available seat hoping they would stop. I was furious. The funny part though was my fury was aimed at myself. "How could I be so stupid as to wear my hair like this? Cute hairstyles were for thin girls, not fat pigs like me.

Don't eat today and things will be better."

By the time I was a teenager, every day started with an ugly battle pitted against myself.

"How many calories did you eat yesterday? Did you go to bed hungry or are you still a gluttonous pig?"

I braced myself for the attack I knew was eminent.

"You're worthless. You're disgusting. You should be ashamed of yourself. When will you get your act together?"

There was a pause and then the meting out of punishment.

"Don't even think about eating today. You get 500 calories – maximum. Your usual hour on the treadmill is now 90 minutes long. You're so disappointing. You better hope no one notices how much fatter you are today than yesterday."

I stood over myself as an unforgiving judge, jury, and executioner each day. This preoccupation with food and my body sucked the joy out of my life. Having never shared my internal world with anyone, I lived a lonely existence. The struggle consumed my life. My mind did not have room for anything else. Everything was pushed to the side for a time in the future when I would be thin and worthy.

I lived my life like this for over thirty years; brutally punishing my own body since its first traumatic violation. As the years passed, frustration and disappointment turned into fury and self-disgust. I felt undeserving of love.

The Miracle Begins

Then, something started to shift. It was barely perceptible at first; more like a tiny whisper from a hidden part of myself. I heard its nurturing wisdom, "Maybe there is another way."

I had been listening to an interview series discussing how the standard American diet affects our brains and made us crave more sugar and other "addictive" foods. I signed up for the series because I thought I would learn how to control my relationship with food. What I ended up learning was the start of something far more valuable. I was introduced to the idea that my dysfunctional relationship with food was caused by something other than my debased lack of willpower and discipline. I began to see that the things I did with food made perfect sense: My eating habits were learned. I didn't really have some incurable disease. I was not a moral miscreant. I was not possessed by the demon of gluttony. I had ingrained habits that I no longer had to let rule me. The answer was not a new diet plan. The answer was self-love.

New daily routines grounded and supported me in discovering this new self. I would spend quiet time alone, journaling, catching old thought patterns, and honouring my true needs...I treated my newly developing practices as sacred rituals. I clung to them to keep me reaching for this new life that I wanted, even when the old patterns threatened to pull me back to the familiar past.

Over time I grew, expanding outwards from someone who would have traded places with *anyone* else on the planet, just so that I wouldn't have to be with myself; into someone who practices radical acceptance and self-love each day.

Sharing the Miracle

I approached my time of healing much like a scientist would. I was very conscious of the neuropathways that were hardwired into my brain and how I could make different choices. I kept journals of my findings and tested them against what various healers and teachers would share. I found a set of core truths that spoke to me, leading me to my healing and transformation. And then, I felt called by an unknown, yet miraculous force, to help others layout their own path to food and body freedom. As if my pen was guided by the source of universal wisdom and grace, I authored a program that serves as a roadmap for others on this journey. Teaching and mentoring have now become my life's purpose.

Today, I have the honor of walking beside other women as they develop a nourishing relationship with food, learn respect for their bodies, and reconnect with their sacred inner wisdom. It's not that I have more wisdom than anyone else, it's only that I've come through to the other side. We never need someone else's wisdom, but sometimes we need someone who will ask us the right questions and put us in touch with our own innate challenges, fears, and doubts. No matter what your challenges may be, I offer you the following suggestions:

    1.   Learn to connect with your highest, truest self, and trust

that self. It has all the answers to all the questions that you could ever ask. Connecting is as simple as tuning into that small, gentle voice that is waiting to be heard.

2. Know that no matter what has happened to you in the past, you are not broken. Your challenges are not a life sentence. You have simply trained your brain in a way that doesn't serve. Training your brain in a way that does serve is entirely possible.

3. Reach out and get help. As Einstein is famous for saying; "We can't solve problems by using the same kind of thinking we used when we created them." Leaning on someone else for a while and gaining a new perspective is a valuable part of the healing process.

4. Believe that change is possible. Believe that things can be different for you. Change takes effort but the work is beautiful even when it is hard.

If you are someone that has unwanted challenges with food, whether that is binge eating, emotional eating, overeating or chronic dieting, I invite you to join my Freedom Channel which is a site full of free resources such as mini-courses, webinars, blogs, and worksheets. You can sign up for this support at the following web address: https://www.freedombynuuaria.com.

Freedom is possible and I stand ready to support you in every way I can.

Yvonne Aileen

Yvonne Aileen is the author of several nonfiction books including the goddess series: *Goddesses Don't Diet: The Girlfriends' Guide to Intermittent Fasting; Goddesses Are Ageless: The Girlfriends' Guide to Health, Happiness, and Vitality at Any Age;* and *Goddesses Stay Sexy: The Girlfriends' Guide to Dating, Relationships, and Sexual Health.* She is the publisher of *800 Muses*, a cooperative publishing house that helps women authors promote and share their stories. Yvonne lives in the Pacific Northwest with her sons, Max and Sam.

*"If you don't share what you're meant to share the people
you're meant to help will continue to suffer."*
~ Yvonne Aileen

Reconstructing the Mosaic

Every little girl wants a pony. I had one. I shared our Shetland, Frosty, with my older sister Kathy. Barely out of toddlerhood, we could jump on her warm back and ride her all over our 11-acre farm, Kathy holding onto Frosty's black mane, me holding onto Kathy. If we ever slipped off, Frosty would wait patiently for us to climb back on. When we were four and five, we rode her in a local parade, Kathy and I in blue jeans, cowboy boots, and western shirts, Frosty's mane and tail adorned with ribbons. Our father walked beside us while our mother looked after our two younger brothers.

An outdoorsman, our dad had wanted a son, but he had to wait through the birth of two girls and two more years before our brother Lance was born, and then Wes the following year. As the second child of disappointing gender, I became my father's tomboy, threading worms onto hooks, climbing trees, stomping oak galls, and trying to be brave when he again convinced me the electric fence wasn't on. "Go ahead, touch it," he would tease.

In the summer, Kathy and I would watch our brothers and drink Kool-Aid out of a mason jar while our mother cleared Scotch broom from the grazing areas. She spent hours yanking out the toxic green stems dotted with yellow flowers while the Kool-Aid got warm, and her children turned pink in the sun.

Our house was a small and sturdy shack with tar paper for siding, well water, and no bathroom. Our parents had the only bedroom and my siblings, and I slept in bunk beds in the hall. Flashlights for Christmas helped with nighttime visits to the outhouse, and we bathed in a galvanised tub in the kitchen. Our vegetable garden produced green beans, corn, radishes, and lettuce, and all four babies cut their teeth on the venison jerky our dad smoked. He was often gone on week-long hunting trips and would return with raccoon, bobcat, deer, and once, a cougar. He brought our two hound dogs with him, and sometimes Thumper, a spaniel mix and family pet who was promoted to hunting companion after our dad accidentally shot him and he survived.

When I was six, our father got a job as a park ranger, and we moved to a larger town. Our new house had three bedrooms and indoor plumbing. We bought our vegetables at the store and our father had less time to hunt. We were able to bring Frosty and Thumper with us but had to board Frosty with a neighbour. Left alone too long, she changed from the docile, patient pony we knew into a dangerous creature we barely recognized. Our parents sold her. Thumper caught distemper and died.

Our dad's new boss had a 19-year-old daughter who worked at the local A&W, and when he took us there for burgers and root beer, she would openly flirt with him. We weren't told right away why our mother moved into a small yellow house in town and couldn't understand why she didn't want to be with us anymore. Later we learned that our father and the A&W girl were having an affair. I was just eight years old when our parents divorced, with Mom getting full custody and the house while our father moved out.

We saw our father every other weekend for roller skating, pizza, the beach, hiking, camping, or bowling. He broke it off with the A&W girl but sometimes introduced us to other women he was dating. It didn't feel right to see him with anyone besides our mother and the weekend adventures felt false like we were all playing a game of make-believe.

After our father moved out, in important ways, our mother also disappeared. She began drinking and dated a carousel of men, leaving us with babysitters, sometimes overnight. A year after our dad left, she became pregnant and hastily married a man who we later learned wasn't the father. Our new brother was Timmy and his real father was someone our mother had met in a bar and only known by a first name.

One day two years after the divorce, when everything was still feeling jagged and unsettled, Mom answered the telephone. I heard her say, "Oh, no! Peggy, no!" and she began sobbing. All five of us kids gathered around her, trying to figure out what had happened, but she was crying so hard that it was hard to make out any words. I thought something bad must have happened to Uncle Jack, Aunt Peggy's husband.

When she finally hung up, Mom looked at us, shock and grief in her eyes. Still crying, she managed to say, "Kids, I have bad news.

Your father has been killed." We held our breath and waited for the lie to be retracted. It was impossible that this man who carried us on his shoulders and threw us into snowbanks and could, with his eyes closed, reach into a coffee can full of broken crayons and pick out the exact color we needed, had been taken from us forever. I could feel myself floating above this scene, distancing myself from the action like a movie camera operator. But when her words sunk in, I was slammed back into reality and we all rushed into our mom's arms crying, even Timmy, who was too young to know what was happening.

The story came out in chapters. Our mother had said "been killed," not "died." We learned our dad had been murdered by a hitchhiker he had offered a lift to, that he'd been shot, rolled into his sleeping bag, and left in a ditch, that the hitchhiker had stolen his car, the window had been shot out and glass and blood were everywhere.

Our father's murder shattered our lives and made us reluctant celebrities in town. When we returned to school, classmates and teachers sympathised while probing for details. Where did this happen? Did they catch the guy? How did you hear about it?

We were thrown into unfamiliar poverty. On the farm, we had been poor but suburban poverty cut deeper. My mother applied for welfare assistance, and we received boxes of food and Christmas gifts from the fire department and hand-me-down clothes from relatives and friends' children. When the bread was on sale, five loaves for a dollar, a limit of five, our mother would send each of us into the store separately and fill our deep freezer. Once we were given a box of oranges and we each ate our fill. I ate nine of them, one after the other, starting each peel with the back of a spoon because I had begun biting my nails to the quick. Nail-biting would become my pacifier and secret shame for the next 30 years. For now, it kept me from screaming.

When we most needed her, our mother checked out. Feeling victimised, her drinking got worse, and we often saw her drunk. On one of her binges, she complained to the neighbour lady that she had nothing left to live for. At that moment, I felt a sharp hatred for her. Wasn't I enough? Weren't we all enough? Wasn't it her job to take care of us?

Over the next five years, we moved from one dreary house to another, often in the middle of a school year. When I turned 12, our grandparents helped us buy a mustard-coloured tract house, and soon after, Mom introduced us to a new stepfather who didn't work but who assumed dominion over our family and expected us to anticipate his needs. He would yell at us children, accuse our mother of having affairs, and without warning, slap us across the head for infractions like getting food on his spoon when serving him. We learned we were at his mercy because our mother would not intervene. He isolated us from our grandparents, and we saw them only during their numerous break-ups that involved broken windows, restraining orders, stalking, and once, the theft and sale of anything of value in our house.

When that marriage, which lasted two years, finally ended, we moved in with our grandparents for several months. One day Mom introduced us to the man who would become our third stepfather. After they married, we moved to a new house and family life became more even keeled, but their coupledom took center stage, with Kathy and I being given the responsibility of looking after our younger brothers. We moved again, several times. Finally, at the beginning of my senior year of high school, I moved out of the home; I had just turned 17. I was glad to control my own destiny, but I felt heavy guilt about leaving my brothers behind, especially when Kathy joined the Army that year and moved away.

As adults, each of my siblings and I patched our lives together as best we could. But, like the time Wes opened all his Christmas presents in the middle of the night and then rewrapped them with masking tape, the patchwork showed. Three of my siblings turned to alcohol. Wes spent two stints in prison for driving while intoxicated. All of us had failed marriages. My nails and cuticles were often bloody and ragged, my teeth were shortened from years of night-time grinding, and I sometimes forced myself to eat even when I wasn't hungry. It felt like I was punishing myself, but I didn't know what for. "Take it, take it, eat it" I would say to myself as I reached for more and more. I also panicked when money wasn't coming in regularly, often working two jobs or a full-time job plus a side business while always searching out new ways to add income. To increase my earning potential, I became the first of my siblings to pursue a bachelor's degree, often quitting to work more hours, then resuming. It took me 11 years, but I finally had it and later, for added good measure, I got my master's.

As to relationships, I became a serial dater, choosing men for security or as father figures rather than for compatibility. I married and divorced twice. The second marriage brought me two beautiful sons. I had become a mother.

After my second marriage ended, I met a man who reminded me so much of my father that even my sister saw it. He was an outdoorsy man's man with a quick wit and a sometimes-ornery sense of humor. I was irresistibly drawn to him, but once we began dating, I found that he was nothing like I'd imagined. He broke promises, was frequently critical, and he allowed his adult children to insult me. It felt like I was slipping backward through time, losing all the protective walls I'd built up around me, that I was at his mercy. But twice, when he tried to be overly strict with my sons, some part of me, I'll call her Girl X, stood up for them. Girl X made sure my sons knew I would never abandon them and would always protect them. Her voice was weak, but she made herself heard when he hurt me, and I acted and broke it off. But almost as soon as he was gone, I was in agony and begging him to come back. I broke up with him 14 times over six years. A friend asked, "Are you just afraid to be alone?" But that wasn't it. I was afraid *for him*, for what might happen to him without me. Even though he didn't seem to need me at all.

I felt my spirit shrink each time we reunited, and I began to question my self-image. What was wrong with me? Why did I want the company of someone who treated me badly? Did I think this was what I deserved? In my darkest moment, I took a steak knife from the kitchen drawer and brought it to my bed. I turned my left arm over, looking at the pale skin, the tight veins. I didn't want to kill myself because I would never leave my sons without a mother. How deep would I need to cut to let the pain out? Then I remembered my boys would be home from their fathers in a couple of hours and the cat would need her eyedrops. It would take two of us to hold her and my sons would see my bandaged wrists and want to know what happened. This was my pain, and I refused to make it theirs. I let the knife drop on the bed. Looking down at this incongruous tableau, Girl X shouted, "ENOUGH!"

I rose from the bed, walked to the kitchen, and put the knife back in the drawer, frightened to think how close I had come to let the pain win.

Now I understand the phrase, "the depth of one's despair." I had hit bottom and bounced back up, but not out. From that moment, I made it my mission to find a way to break the cycle I was in. I read relationship books and spiritual books and attended seminars. I consulted psychics, astrologers, energy healers, past life regressionist, hypnotists, and counselors. But still, I was unable to end the relationship because the grief I experienced when I turned away from this man was so profound. It was, as one counselor noted, "like you're tapping into some other grief." It's hard to see the forest for the trees when you're the wildfire.

My search for answers finally led me to a spiritual retreat where a chance remark brought brilliant clarity. *"I was acting out my mother's story, thinking I could change the ending."* Because my boyfriend reminded me so strongly of my father, I had equated our separation with my parent's divorce, which had been followed by my father's murder. The splintered child in me believed that if I could save that relationship, I could save my parents' marriage, save my father's life, and erase our family trauma.

Carl Jung said, *"Until you make the unconscious conscious, it will direct your life, and you will call it fate."* All the counseling and spiritual work I'd done up to that point had been more salve than salvation. It took understanding *why* I was in this destructive cycle to break it and finally let that little girl off the hook. She didn't cause the trauma, and she couldn't fix it by remaining in a destructive relationship.

This was the beginning of my healing, my journey to me. There was still work to do but now I had the answers I needed to take the steps to thrive.

In *The Body Keeps Score*, Bessel van Der Kolk writes, *"Beneath the surface of the protective parts of trauma survivors there exists an undamaged essence, a Self that is confident, curious, and calm, a Self that has been sheltered from destruction by the various protectors that have emerged in their efforts to ensure survival. Once those protectors trust that it is safe to separate, the self will spontaneously emerge, and the parts can be enlisted in the healing process."*

It was time for me to rediscover myself. One by one, I began taking apart the patched-together shards of my story and piecing them together into a clear, integrated picture.

Xena's Path to Integration

* * *

I started by making a timeline of my life, documenting significant family events. By revisiting the major events in my life, I was able to recognise the source of the soul wounds that continued to hurt me. I could also recognise the gifts they brought.

I began to untangle all my feelings—guilt, shame, anger, embarrassment, and fear—and then I acknowledged and accepted them. I took ownership of what was mine to take without blaming myself or others. I fully recognized the connection between my relationship with my boyfriend and my family trauma. I understood why I had allowed this toxic relationship to continue, which released its hold on me. I knew the role I played in it and why, and I knew it was up to me to stop playing it. I forgave myself and I also forgave my boyfriend who I'd cast in a leading role in the sequel to a movie he'd never seen. He would never be my father, and I could never recover my father's love through him. I am grateful for that relationship because it was the catalyst to unlocking my past.

Today I no longer look for someone to rescue or protect me, because I can do that for myself. Instead, I look for men who have done their own inner work and who have no need to conquer or control me.

I recognise my own strength and power. In the past, whenever I would take on a traditional male project, such as changing a light fixture, painting a house, or resetting a toilet, I would jokingly refer to myself as Xena, Warrior Princess. I now claim her spirit and strength. Xena *is* Girl X; her qualities are authentically me and always have been, even before my tomboy days.

I looked at my relationship with food and began to research and experiment with intermittent fasting for health, weight loss and maintenance, and longevity. I learned to control when I eat, how much, and what. I've completed several extended fasts and love the freedom and sense of control fasting brings.

I looked at my finances and made friends with money, recognising that, like food, its only energy, neither good nor bad. I've learned to relax more and work less, but this is still a work in progress.

Next, I sought out and added affirming people to my life, women, and men of integrity and character. My family's many moves and starting over in new schools taught me how to open my heart to new connections. I helped a Unity Church minister turn seven years of devotional blogs into a beautiful book,

Proceed As Way Opens, as a gift for her 90th birthday. It has helped so many find peace. I regularly practice self-care, self-compassion, and self-love. I meditate and practice breathwork.

I have also led and love participating in beach clean-ups, and I pick up litter wherever I go. My dad, the former park ranger, would be proud.

Importantly, I've forgiven my mother. I know she did the best she could, given her life's circumstances and her very young age (she was just 17 when she married our father). I now see her as an astonishingly strong woman who loved her children fiercely. After she passed in 2000, I inherited her mother's ring and I wear it whenever I need to feel her strength.

Have I resolved all my childhood trauma? No, but the pieces are back together, the picture is clear, and I'm whole and thriving.

Elizabeth Gilbert wrote, "If you don't share what you're meant to share, the people you're meant to help will continue to suffer." Everyone has a story. I make it a practice to listen to others' stories and to share what I know, especially the hard-earned lessons. I love my life.

Sue Holmes

Sue Holmes is from England and lives in Sintra, Portugal. She is recognized as a 'Master Healer/Teacher', who runs her own center for wellness and transformation, offering deep healing sessions, Feng Shui, and space clearing (in person and online). Sue is founder of 'The Modern Shaman Academy' with accredited courses: 'Shamanic Practitioner & Energy Healer' and 'Space Clearing & Geomancy Consultant'. She is a medicine woman, mystic and mentor. A writer, songwriter and singer, Sue's debut album is 'Heaven on Earth'. Find her at https://firehorse.uk.com

"Beauty grows from healing trauma.
It shines in our presence, creativity, and passionate service".
- Sue Holmes

Discovering Treasure in the Wreckage

A massive, powerful, black serpent enters my mouth, travels through my body, and comes out between my legs, coiling back again, violating my lower and upper mouths in a relentless, unholy figure-of-eight, whilst I'm floundering desperately in a swimming pool, out of my depth, in the dark. I am terrified because I cannot escape and I'm dying. This is the recurring nightmare I experienced throughout my childhood, youth and into my thirties.

I come from a caring, old-fashioned, middle-class family and grew up within a simple, sheltered, rural setting. Playing in the village school playground, cantering on imaginary horses, escaping from 'baddies', I suggest "Let's play, they take off our clothes and tie us up". When my real-life pony Rudolph bucks and rears beneath me however, I beg my Dad not to let go of the reins, sobbing "I'm useless, I'm rubbish". I adore my pony but sometimes something takes hold of me and I whip him furiously.

As a teenager, I appear outspoken and confident to others.While helping my Mum in the garden, at the sudden sight of long white roots, I cringe and run off across the lawn shuddering with disgust. I can't bear my neck to be touched. I cry before my bedroom mirror, "God, why did you make me ugly?"

At boarding school, I'm lying in the dark, in the cramped dormitory, listening to the sounds of breathing. It sounds creepy. A feeling of panic and terror grows inside me until wet with sweat, heart pounding with emergency, the floodgates open. I thrash around as tears and screams pour out, "Help! Help!" over and over. Inconsolable, hyper-ventilating and semi-conscious, I'm carried to hospital. My concerned parents, teachers and doctors are baffled.

At a school fancy-dress disco, everyone is open-mouthed, when from amongst the fairies and princesses, I emerge in a revealing dominatrix outfit, vigorously thrashing the floor with a huge whip. I shop-lift hordes of clothes and alcohol, "the only thing I can't steal is cigarettes' I boast. Disassociated, I under-achieve at school. When I leave home, I'm depressed, a binge-drinker and I comfort-eat in secret, hide the wrappers, gorging on chocolate and carbs until I'm physically bursting and tormented with guilt and shame.

I live in crusty, druggie London squats and go out with punks and rebels. My relationships are a series of fight, flight, and freeze responses when being around nudity or seeing images of a sexual nature. We are watching a comedy film on TV, when a woman's breast is exposed, horror erupts within me. I shout angrily at my boyfriend and housemate and run out in blind terror, as fast and far away as I can, into the night, through a London housing estate. My partner catches up with me, "What's wrong Sue? This isn't you?"

Cold, exhausted and crying, I eventually agree to come home. I lie trembling under the covers, unable to speak or bear being touched for days.

I am hyper-vigilant, desperate to control events to avoid exposure to nudity: I refuse to watch TV; censoring everything we watch or read and avoiding swimming. I'm paranoid in case there are hidden cameras when I undress. No one can understand what is causing this. One minute I'm 'normal': relaxed and vivacious and the next, I'm overtaken by a tsunami of cold terror, a wasteland of worthlessness, a volcano of burning rage, and a landslide of despair. It's an agonising mystery, even to me.

Taking Ecstasy pills and dancing at rave parties, is unifying, euphoric and fun, but also a melancholy escape into a stupor of rushes, lights and beats. Then finding a way to cope with its inevitable serotonin-depleted crash landings, I naively smoke Heroin for a couple of years and end up zonked out, skinny and defeated. My only lifelines were the comfort of dogs, music, going for walks in nature and a trusted friend I confide in.

To escape this relentless cycle of hopelessness, I fly away to explore India. With a sense of nothing to lose and nothing to come back to, I enjoy incredible adventures. My lowest point is in Bangkok, aged twenty-eight, when something possesses me to sample Thai Heroin. One night, I over-dose and stop breathing. I come around again to see anxious faces hovering over me as I am held under a cold shower. One of the guys who saves my life also ransacks my room, stealing my passport and money. It is a wake-up call.

I land back in the UK, still feeling lost. A friend recommends

Reiki. I am determined to do something to shift my state. I am surviving on unemployment benefit, so to pay for the course, I don't eat for a week. Once I am attuned to Reiki, and with daily self-healing, I feel like a car that's shifted up a gear. Over the next twenty-five years, I gradually replace parties with ceremonies, travelling abroad with inner transformation, drugs and alcohol with plant spirit medicine and truck-driving with my own holistic services. Dowsing alone at a Derbyshire stone circle, I smile as a moment of serendipity dawns: Yes! I have found my true vocation, working with natural magic!

Socially I'm a friendly extrovert and party animal, play-fighting, laughing, and dancing on tables, wearing sparkly tops. But in relationships with men, they discover there is a hidden, contradictory, and broken side to me.

I blame my boyfriends for these devastating panic attacks until I eventually realize they are just a trigger for them. I dread the reactions: tension; confusion; aggression. It's all I can do to survive these episodes with my sanity intact. In those moments when it overtakes me, I huddle myself into a blanket, shrinking into the sofa, silently repeating "I'm safe, I'm loved". I struggle to breathe through the paralysis and explosion of panic, fury, and terror, until it subsides. In the midst of this, I see images of faces snarling, eyes glaring.

"For fuck's sake! What's wrong with you?"

I try to say "I don't know, I don't know" but my mouth is locked tight and the words won't come out. I'm desolate and adrift with no refuge.

Since my early twenties, I have attempted to work with conventional therapists. They all proclaim I have PTSD (from what we can't establish) and although we try to find strategies for recovery, nothing changes. I feel like a hopeless case and entertain suicidal thoughts. My doctor prescribes Prozac, an anti-depressant, which only makes me feel subdued and couldn't-care-less about running up credit card debt. I try every healing method I can, each one a step of progress and then I'm triggered again, sliding backwards like the children's board game of 'Snakes and Ladders'. The only therapist who ever mentions abuse to me directly, is one of the UK's most respected iridologists, who says he can see sexual abuse took place when I was age three. At the time I shrug it off, "Not as far as I remember" I say.

At first, my lack of trust and self-doubt gets in the way of my training to become a healer. I often leave the room in tears because I can't sense much. I never imagine I will be teaching it one day. The key to the door of my breakthrough finally arrives from the plant kingdom, composed of vines, leaves, roots and Cacti, a tremendous gift for which I am eternally grateful. Their medicine is a harrowing ordeal mixed with blissful pleasure, bringing deep healing and profound teachings. They cleanse my system, reveal my innate gifts and re-awaken my senses. I become a shamanic practitioner and seer before I access my core wound. In hindsight, I can see that the timing was divinely orchestrated so that I had the stability and skills to process what finally emerged.

At forty-nine years of age, working at a healing retreat in Wales, blessed by the power of the solstice sun, and the safety of community, I am noticing how much love I feel for everyone and everything, which brings up the question in my mind: "So, why don't I feel lovable?" It didn't make sense.

It is while I'm facilitating a healing for someone around their childhood sexual abuse, that I stop abruptly as a wave of darkness and nausea clouds my focus. I excuse myself and move away into my own space. I feel a weight pulsing in my solar plexus. It's hard to budge, but with the aid of self-massage and a snuff of 'Hapé' tobacco, I finally vomit. As I purge, I see a face that I hadn't thought of for many years. He is way off my radar, since he died when I was six years old; it is my paternal grandfather. He is showing me a bondage-style pornographic magazine. Demons are coming out of his eyes. I feel like a little girl again, crying and trembling in shock.

My world stands still with the enormity of the realisation that some kind of sexual abuse took place with him, when I was very young. As I make the connections, all the pennies drop and my entire life starts to make sense. This is why I have anxiety at the sight of nudity and have massive trust issues and feel so worthless.

Even though it is horrific and a sordid 'can of worms' to open, I know it is better than staying in that relentless 'washing machine' of PTSD and the purgatory of not knowing why. I feel saner than I ever have before; coupled with a sense of relief, knowing now that I have clarity, I can begin to heal the trauma and reclaim my life.

Since that day, working with different practitioners and natural healing techniques, I continued to gain insight into specific and intense moments of torturous abuse. I purge and cry, shake my limbs and punch pillows, releasing the sounds and emotions that have been suppressed for forty-six years. They are visceral body memories, the kind that prickle my hairs and run shivers down my spine. Memories of the mind are less reliable, but strong experiences are held in the body. Our bodies know the truth and we can trust their wisdom.

I am vigilant to record the details exactly as I remember them. My grandfather is a sadist. He shows me pornography and then 'punishes me' and takes photographs. Throat-bound, naked, threatened with a stick, I'm trembling with terror. He makes me eat his feces. I sense that my grandmother is there, keeping watch, lest my parents return. Betrayal stings the back of my heart.

Now my recurring, figure-of-eight snake nightmare makes sense, as I recall being tied up and abused at both ends simultaneously. In that moment, I stop breathing and surrender to death. It feels intensely lonely and black. I am led to a windy cliff-edge. Two tall beings stand in front of me shimmering with light and showering me with love.

"Not now Sue, it's not time".

I am pulled back into my body. My grandparents are shaking and splashing me with water, panic-stricken. I have a near-death experience at the age of three and they are spared the crime of murder.

Wisdom of the Wounded Healer

Opening up a long-buried, childhood abuse story is extremely challenging in several ways. First, there is the pain of re-living and processing the shock, terror and shame of the inner child who blocked it out because it was 'too painful to go there'. Secondly, we need to continue to function, work and take care of our adult responsibilities. Then there is the fear and ramifications of sharing such a truth-bomb with family and friends; unable to predict their reaction or protect them from their process.

In my experience as a healer, families may be devastated and heart-broken; angry and defensive; or in denial, since it's too frightening and shameful to accept and with so much invested in it not being true, they refuse to listen. Some may reject a story that comes without proof and choose to adhere to favorable memories. You may receive the kindness and support you need, finding ways to grieve and heal together, or conversely find yourself disbelieved and ostracised, suffering another betrayal. It is possible that the act of sharing it may be judged more severely than the abuse. I recommend that before sharing with those people who are likely to get upset, make sure you feel strong enough to deal with their reaction, whatever that might be.

What is the other option? To stay silent and take these grisly secrets to our graves? Abuse has been hidden for thousands of years, with the victims silenced as a symptom of patriarchal oppression, which lingers in all of us. We need whistle-blowers. With so many lies and deceptions in the fabric of society, every expression of honesty is valuable in reweaving a more authentic collective consciousness.

I wouldn't share my story without being utterly convinced of its validity. It's true in every cell of my heart, soul, womb, guts, brains and bones. It makes sense of every nuance of my entire life. With my throat unleashed, I need to speak out: transforming tragedy into inspiration, victim to mentor. I fear the repercussions; but candidly sharing my experience, however revealing, upsetting or controversial, is more responsible than protecting dark secrets.

It would be easy to remain bitter about how these festering wounds, that had been unconsciously running me all these years, have sabotaged my life. However, I feel guided to see that from a spiritual perspective, this was meant to be. In a dream, Owl says bluntly: "No matter what your grandfather did, he is your teacher". This is my karma and initiation to my purpose: to experience this trauma so that I can become part of the healing of abuse, for my soul, my bloodline and the collective.

No doubt, my grandfather was acting out abuse that he had received and that helps me to have compassion for him, but my inner child took longer to feel that way. She feels present and raw for the first few years since that memory box opened. I let the wise, adult parts of myself hold space for my wounded child, supporting her healing process. It takes a while for me to feel it whole-heartedly, but eventually in a cacao ceremony, I sense his spiritual presence and remorse, and in a moment of grace, respond, "I'm ok now and I forgive you".

How did I get to be OK? The first step is safety. I find skilled people I trust to hold space for me. It helps to speak with a rape-crisis counsellor, but I don't talk or think my way out of sexual trauma, it requires many sessions of deep shamanic energy healing, sound-therapy, massage, breath-work and natural medicines. Some may prefer to find coping mechanisms rather than open wounds up for healing; but in my experience, the only way out is through, and this can be a tough yet rewarding journey.

I have to become vulnerable and allow my heart to feel it. Many times, I'm trembling all over, wailing and gasping for breath, drowning in a repulsive stew of evil, horror, shame and insanity. It's intense, dark and overwhelming. Eventually, it clears and the light returns. In its place, I reclaim the gems of my authentic essence with 'soul retrieval': innocence, self-esteem, sexuality, voice, wildness and dignity. The once-feared serpent has now transformed into a potent ally.

My daily practice is 'Walking the Lemniscate', a moving meditation via the infinity symbol which I walk with an intention to integrate polarities, explore possibilities; or simply find my way back to balance. The figure-of-eight shape that appeared in my recurring nightmare became my path to healing, spiritual growth and natural ecstasy. Dancing, singing, art and writing are essential for me, not only as a way to feel alive, sensual and expressive, but to tune back into beauty, magic and the divine. We say 'laughter is the best medicine' and it surely lifts our spirits.

Since this core wound was exposed my life has dramatically transformed. For a start, I treated myself to a forty-nine-inch TV! I now relax and enjoy films, without fear of nude scenes. From the wreckage of who I was, many treasures have been discovered: creativity, abundance, community, spiritual awakening, peace in my core and worthwhile service for all. My career took off, I was thrilled to record an album of my own songs and I've penned a magical realism memoir. I'm still a 'work in progress', but I know how far I have come and all the energy and imagination that was previously drained by trauma and victim consciousness is now channeled into creativity with enthusiasm.

Heroine of my own ordeals, how could I not share all this transformation with others, who may be feeling as wretched, hopeless and messed up as I once did? As 'wounded healers', all the traumas we have experienced can become alchemized into embodied wisdom to hold space for others.

There are many options for healing techniques; search for the right method and practitioner for you. A cautionary note is that, as with all walks of life, not all facilitators are trustworthy, so choose carefully. There are even predatory narcissists, disguised by the glamour of altruism, spirituality and credible associates, who target empaths. You might avoid a regrettable encounter by familiarising yourself with the associated terminology and red flags: love-bombing, devaluation, gas-lighting, entitlement, victimhood, abuse and smear campaigns about ex's or critics. They manipulate people by exploiting insecurities, loyalty, compassion, making them feel special and offering attractive opportunities. They appear convincing, with knowledge, skills or charm, look the part and talk the talk, but lack integrity, empathy, accountability and eventually stories of misconduct emerge. However, the words of a victim of abuse may be doubted, whilst the perpetrator acts like the victim of injustice and cultivates defenders. Be discerning, research their reputation beyond their closest supporters, don't put anyone on a pedestal, maintain your autonomy, trust your gut-instincts and if anything feels off, just leave.

The process of awakening can reveal to us our shadows, those aspects that are hidden from our awareness. The bright shadows remind us of our beauty, power, divinity: to be our unique selves, with no apologies! The dark shadows remind me of the saying, 'when you point one finger at another, there are three pointing back at you'. The darkest aspects of humanity run as subconscious traces within us all - and have been repeating through eons of time, through the cause and effect of ancestral and karmic patterns of violence, abuse and exploitation. Like the Hawaiian Ho'oponopono prayer, with responsibility, love, forgiveness and gratitude, we can address and heal these traumas. It takes people who have the heart, integrity and awareness to break the cycles, to carry the flame of truth and let our longing for redemption and primal roar for justice and freedom, ignite passion for change.

Lisa Cleminson Grezo

I am an authenticity seeker continuously exploring ways of finding my own truth. I am in awe of the power and wisdom the body holds. I love sharing my experiences and modalities with one-to-one clients and groups. I am a Tantric Journey Educator, Somatic Consent Empowerment Facilitator, Clarity Breathwork Practitioner, TRE Practitioner, and Holistic Pelvic Care Practitioner. I am particularly interested in connecting to the sacred medicine that is within every one of us. We are not broken, just disconnected from our truth. I also sell sacred healing tools and courses for women at tantrictools.co.uk. Website lisa-grezo.com.

"AUTHENTICITY: The daily practice of letting go who we think we are supposed to be, and embracing who we are"
~ Brené Brown

Romancing the Shadows

I am looking at photographs from my childhood; they seem to help me remember. Or, maybe I am just constructing a story about what I am seeing, as now witnessed by my adult self. I notice the smile I learned to put on, and as I write, I feel the sadness rise up inside and my tears slowly gather. I take a sip of coffee and enjoy the warm, milky sensation in my mouth and all the way inside my body as I swallow. A tear rests on the left side of my right eye. I don't remember a lot from my childhood.

My earliest memory of my dad has my stomach pulsating. As the energy moves upwards from my belly, it stiffens my shoulders and sets off a sharp pain between my shoulder blades. I remember the smell of food cooking and warm air against my face, but my body feels cold. I feel stuck, I can't move, I am petrified. My dad is standing in front of the open door of my wardrobe. He bellows at me, "I am going to play holy war with you for not cleaning your room properly. You have hidden things in your cupboard instead of tidying up as I told you!" My body starts shaking and I sob. I am 6 years old.

It's Mum's birthday. She is opening her gift, which my seven-year-old hands have so carefully wrapped in paper. She is seated on a chair, while I stand barefoot on the carpet in front of her, watching with anticipation. I look at her face when she sees the present. I know something is wrong. Her face stiffens as she looks at the present and then at me. My stomach is pulsating now, my heart beats faster, my mouth and my back feels tight. She raises her voice in disgust, "Why are you giving me your old sunglasses? You have put no thought into this present, you are just giving me something you don't want! You are selfish. I don't want this present from you."

I hated my early school years. On Sunday evenings I would sit in the living room armchair and watch TV series, wrapped in heaviness and dread with a stone sitting in my stomach. I tried so hard to get it right at school and still, I kept getting told off for getting it wrong. Dinner time made me feel trapped and sick at being forced to eat everything on my plate. A rare highlight of school was discovering my first love when a boy named Richard said: "I like your fish". It was crafted from two white paper plates and when I had compared it to the others in the classroom I had noticed how much better theirs were than mine. His words surprise me so much, that I froze. Afterward, I would relish his words, I would daydream about him and what other nice things he could be saying to me; I would always look out for him at school.

I'm 17 and in my first relationship. Michael is beautiful, kind, and caring. I feel so lucky. He is my first experience with sex, which is beautiful. It was also my first experience with jealousy, which was not so beautiful. I am leaning into his body watching tv with him in my bedroom. I feel warm, cozy, and safe. Suddenly my body tightens, my heart beats faster and I feel as though I am being punched in the stomach. On the screen, the music video 'Girls on Film' by Duran Duran comes on. The voices in my head compare me with the beautiful models, looking so sexy, with perfect bodies and perfect faces. "*He wants them. They are far prettier than you. You should be like them, then you would be perfect*". I swallow my breath. I need to get away but I can't move. I stay through the video and feel the pain, which is debilitating. When I can, I escape to the toilet where my body starts to relax slightly. I know there is something wrong with me. I feel ashamed.

My internal navigation system was always on, scanning my environment to see if there are any threats to me: someone more intelligent, funny or in any way, I judged 'better' than me. There is something about attractiveness however that topped my 'better' list and I would constantly compare my body with other women. After gaining five kilograms, I told my mum one day that I was going to lose weight. She agreed that it was a good idea.

This was the beginning of my six-year journey with anorexia. I weighed myself several times a day, terrified of putting on weight. Every time I lost more weight, I felt an incredible sense of achievement. Food consumed my thoughts, along with how many calories I had eaten. I lost more weight and didn't have a period for 6 years. Christmas 1991 I spent alone. I told my family I was unwell, which was a lie. I didn't want to eat, and I didn't want to be confronted. The next day, I woke up alone in bed. Putting my hand on my ribs, I felt my bones against my palm. I move my hand to my back, feeling the fuzzy, soft down my body had grown in self-protection. I didn't like the feel of it, I felt angry, I wanted it to go away. And I felt sad, so sad that I was here all alone; wanting someone to come and make me feel better.

Suddenly I realised that I had two choices: I could continue like this, getting thinner, becoming weaker to finally die; or I could start eating and choose life. I chose life.

Life has taken me on many adventures along with the familiar themes that ran my childhood and teens. Looking back, it is a litany of seeking approval from others, a constant sense of desperation to 'get things right' and to be right. I had to perform to fit into an image of what I believed others would approve of me. I had no needs of my own. I would say yes to everything. I would give everyone what they wanted, even an employer who would touch me inappropriately once helping himself to me while on a business trip to Denmark. It was a scene I didn't feature in; I was numb and far removed.

I had a curiosity for sex, always feeling something was missing. I would Google female orgasm knowing that I was capable of more than just a clitoral orgasm. It led me to exploring tantra and started a deep journey within my own body where I learned much about sexuality. But it also brought me another wake-up call.

I reconnected a year later with a fellow student with whom I received? from, during our training. He then asked me if I wanted to practice healing sexuality with him. He planned to stay over with me while on his trip visiting the UK. I refused and said that I wasn't ready and that I first needed to go deeper within myself, before letting anyone in.

I picked him up at the station and took him back to my tiny wooden cottage. We sat on the floor opposite each other, the cottage was starting to warm up, but it was still cold. I looked into his eyes and asked him, "What do you want from me? I felt my belly pulsating again and I noticed my heartbeat increase. My mouth was dry, and my throat felt swollen. Holding both my hands, he looked into my eyes and said, "I don't want anything from you." I felt my body soften; the room felt warmer. I felt so relieved, tears filled my eyes and streamed down my face. I felt safe. Later, I complained about a sore lower back and asked if he was willing to massage it. He poured warm oil on my back, and I felt his hands moving over my skin. I felt myself sinking into deep relaxation. He moved down and massaged my bottom; I sighed with pleasure. I felt his erection and I realised he was aroused. Out of nowhere, he penetrated me. I jerked away in shock; he was out as soon as he was in. I was in disbelief. I felt angry and I felt sad. The sadness felt safer for me, and I started crying. He sat next to me not sure how to react. He eventually said, "When was the last time you had fun when you had sex?" Instead of telling him to fuck off and throwing him out the door, I replied: "Yes, you are right, sex for me these days is not much fun."

I felt ashamed, I felt as though there was something wrong with me. I felt that sex should be fun; that I should be a sex goddess; that I should enjoy sex on demand. We slept in separate beds but the following morning I let him into my bed, I kissed him, and let him masturbate between my legs. I hugged him before taking him back to the station. I did this because a small part of me still wanted him to like me.

It took me four years to say the word rape. I first used the words 'penetration without consent' thinking I was protecting him; now I see I was protecting myself from feeling the pain of owning that I was raped. Writing now, I have to pause. My upper back and throat are tight, tears prickle, hot, and ready to be released. I feel shame wash over me, that this happened. The voice in my head admonishes me, "*you should have been more boundaried, awake, enlightened, stronger, then this would not have happened*". I see how the 'not good enough' wants to blame me for what happened. Logically, I am aware that there is also a story that it wasn't really rape but I am clear. For my body, it was rape, no matter what the story might say.

A large part of my healing has been being able to own that experience. The ability to share MY truth, how MY body feels, and to honor every part of me.

It was this experience that gave me the power to stop looking outside myself but to rather focus on seeing myself more clearly. Instead of being the victim, I chose to own that my distrust in men was reflected in what I had been attracting into my life; that it was me not taking full responsibility for my part. I have spent most of my life in a freeze and fawn? (as in ingratiate) state and I now choose to move away from it.

Each day, I look deeper into myself. I also enjoy the privilege of working as a Somatic Consent Empowerment Facilitator which has had an enormous impact on my life. I interact with conscious men and communities which supports me to heal the fear and distrust I have of men. I am also able to see how it works the other way. Many men have been manipulated by women and men. By bringing our shadows to the light we can see more clearly, both sides of the coin, and have love and compassion for it all. Our survival strategies kept us safe back then; now we can choose to live life out of the shadow.

Working with consent, I have come to understand that there is only consent if an agreement is in place. There need to be clear agreements around who the action is for, rather than just going along with or assuming the other person knows what is right for me. If someone does something without my consent, it puts me in shadow behavior too. My shadow behavior is one of rescuer, do-gooder, doormat, and victim which came from trying to please others, get it right, and be liked. I realize I only have a clear yes when I have a clear no. When I am 100% honest about what is going on inside me, I can trust myself; and those around me can trust me too.

Conscious, connected breath has been an important part of my healing process. It switches my thinking mind off and I can see through the illusions to the truth of what is. I like to say our breath is our own sacred medicine, we get exactly what we need. Shorter breathwork practices are part of my daily self-care and every week I do a longer practice. I continuously feel into what my body needs, be it movement, breath, touch, or something else completely different.

I am responsible for my experience; the world is simply reflecting the stories within me. These stories were not what I chose and were often unconscious. I now hold the knowledge to consciously be the sovereign being I want to be in my life. It's a lifelong journey but today, I am able to speak my truth to others, even though I may fear their judgment. I recently noticed a part of me that wanted to cheat my business partner. I felt ashamed and worried about how she would judge me, fearing that she wouldn't trust me. The opposite happened, she told me she trusts and respects me even more for sharing my vulnerable truth.

As I take time to slow down, feel myself and create safety in my body, I notice how much pleasure is available. I am able to feel energy and vibration in every cell of my body and all around me. If there is any tension, pain, numbness, or judgment in my body, I connect to it with love and compassion. I am able to notice that when I am upset, that I am being set up; that something from the past is triggering me. Now, instead of blaming, I use my breath to go deep within to unravel the truth. I often find that when I am triggered some need is not being met. I am kind and compassionate to all parts of me. And, yes, I do forget, fuck up, get distracted and I do my best to forgive myself and accept that I am a human doing the best I can.

I am grateful for the experiences I have encountered which gave me the fuel to move forward.

My feelings of unworthiness called me to write this story. My own unworthiness overpowered me when I was anorexic, almost eating me up. The power has diminished but it continues to sneak into many areas of my life. When they do, I have to ride the storm and allow it to move through me, remembering that I am not the wound; that it is not true that I am unworthy. Too often, we withdraw from the world because of shame. We keep it to ourselves and many of us suffer because it is unconscious; we are not aware of it. I knew I had a message to share with my story and that it was time for my trauma wound to serve instead of hinder. By romancing our shadows, we can heal them together in a community. We can't do it all alone.

Waking Up the Hands

I would like to share a practice that I hope can help you connect more deeply to yourself by dropping you out of your head and into your skin. It's very simple and brings you into a deep state of calm and connection. Find a comfortable position, leaning back slightly, so your body knows it is relaxing. Place a cushion on your lap and find an object, it doesn't matter what the object is. Notice how you feel in your body right now. Set a timer for between 5 and 10 minutes. Very slowly (you feel more when you slow down) explore the object with your hands. Move your hands over the object or, holding the object in one hand, move the object over the other hand. Keep your attention on the sensations in your fingers and hands. Let thoughts, feelings, and emotions arise if they do, but keep your focus on the experience of your hands. You can be curious and explore your whole hand, wrist, between the fingers, fingertips, and even the back of your hand against the object. Remember to keep your movements unhurried while you explore the touch and feel of your object. Afterward, notice how you are feeling.

Olga Brooks

Olga Brooks is the founder of The Return. An international bestselling author.
Olga's mission is to restore femininity to its original essence by guiding and reminding women
who they truly are. Through Rapid Transformational Therapy, Olga is helping to shift women's
inner world, restoring health, emotional stability, and creating happiness while empowering them
by returning to the wisdom of the heart. She is a sound Reiki healer.
"It's time to redefine the language of equality. Women are not equal. We are the most valuable
part of this life. We are the one's giving life. We are the beauty, the past, the present and the
future." https://thereturntomyfeminineself.today/

"Balance is an essence of harmony.
And only in harmony you will find true happiness."
~ Olga Brook

The Point of No Return

Have you ever experienced a life event so momentous in its shift that you are able to look back and say, "I can never return to the life I once knew"?

Discoveries and realisations come at full price but the knowledge and abilities I have gained remain priceless.

Like most of you, I have undergone tragedies and health problems in my life but the event I am talking about crawled silently into my psyche to become a daily reminder that what I had chosen as good, and right was destroying me piece by piece. Until one day, it left me no choice but to return to my soul space and restore the life I was born to live.

I pick up the phone and dial my mother in Russia. It is not our usual coffee and daily check-in call, this time I have a question burning in my mind. "How old was I when you gave me away to my grandparents?" I blurt out. "You were about 18 months old," she replies. In an attempt to explain, she continues. "You had constant ear infections and we had to stay in the hospital so much. My boss told me to do something about it or else he said, they don't need me there anymore."

I gaze down at my firstborn; a son born here in the USA, and panic, fear, and anger flood through me. How could you have left me when I was so small, at a time when I needed your care and love? This is not the first time in my life that I feel abandoned and alone.

I picture the day. I am a fat cheeked baby, with large gray eyes. I am being bundled into a coat, hat, with a shawl over it all, and mittens. Alighting from the train, the platform is full of villagers waiting to greet their family who has come to visit on the train. "Whose will you be?" they ask curiously as we alight; meaning whose family do you belong to? And we proudly name my grandparents' family's name." Will you be Luda, and this is your Olga?"

If we depart the platform to the right, we will arrive at my mom's parents. To the left is the way to my dad's parents. If there are no freight trains blocking the way, it is easy enough to cross the railway tracks. But there it was, a long train. There is no way to walk around the train and you never know how long you have to wait for it to start moving. The only way to get across is to go under the train. It seems like a quick thing to do; just duck under the train and it is done. But the fear is always there. What if it starts moving? We walk along the dirt road for a while, I am still holding mom's hand. I am getting tired and scared of the cows and dogs that are barking at every house we walk past. Mom carries me most of the way. She is tired herself, managing the bags and me and navigating around the puddles. But this is the solution to her problems at work. My three-year-old brother comes with us that day, but he returns home with her, and I stay behind.

This part of the village has two rows of around twenty houses. My grandparents' house is the third at the end on the right-hand side. There are two wells set in the middle. One looks like a bird. The other well looks like witches live in it.

My grandparents have a cow, a dog, geese, and chickens to take care of. I love cats the most. The kittens are impossible to catch. They are wild and hiss when I try to catch them.

My grandpa likes to hold me on his knee and call me Olga Korbut while I happily bounce up and down. I do not know she is a famous Russian gymnast until I get bigger. In winter, the floors in the house are cold. In the cellar potatoes, canned food, and other winter vegetables are kept stored. The kitchen floors are dusty where mud has been walked indoors. The living room floor is covered with woven runners made from shredded cotton fabric. They are simple and very colourful.

The best part about winter is the brick stove where grandma cooks soups, potatoes, and grain porridge. It heats the whole house and is big enough for me to climb on top of it and sleep there when it is really cold. At night, I lie in the dark and listen to the clock ticking. I cannot understand why mom left me here; I miss her. Even when I am reunited with my family again at the age of three, I feel like I have missed her my whole life.

Throughout my childhood, I continue to spend summers here and with my other grandparents. I feel happy. Together with the local children, we run free in the fields, playing games until nightfall. We gather wild strawberries in the woods and mash them with sugar and eat them with bread and fresh milk. We collect mushrooms, blackberries, blueberries, raspberries, and hazelnuts.

I finish school, college, and go onto university. I became an accountant which was very prestigious for a girl to be at that time in Russia.

When the Soviet Union collapses, the 90th bring many hardships. It is then that I decide to change my destiny and move to the United States. No, it was not easy.

At the age of twenty-two, I became a Russian bride. Moving to the United States of America, I had a lot to learn, including a new language, culture, and the way of living in a new family. This union was short-lived with its own long story, but I knew in my heart that my future is here in the USA.

I choose my second partner and future husband and we settle in to grow a family.

After seven years of marriage, I feel as if I am still learning about American culture, not realising I am on a journey of learning about myself. I am a proud mother of two baby boys living in the suburbs of Boston. But something is missing. Without the care and intimacy required from both partners, my days become more isolated and lonelier, and I worry about the future of my marriage.

I attend church regularly and begin seeing a psychologist. "Abandonment issue?" I am shocked. But it all makes sense. I realize I have struggled with it all my life. It has been tough making friends here. I love people and want a large circle of friends, but I feel alone and further isolated when my husband travels away on regular business trips.

My job is clearly cut out for me. I am there to take care of the babies and manage the household. I kept myself busy in the garden. I make clothes. I paint my babies' rooms. But I feel hurt, confused, and unloved. As the boys grow, my role is less demanding and my place in the family diminishes. My husband continues to climb the corporate ladder and becomes more distant. I turned into a moth with no wishes, no dreams, or permission for either. I am cut off from intimacy and resources. Until the day comes when I don't know who I am. I am lost in myself with no way of knowing what I like or don't like. What I should wish for or not. I lose the vision of my life and I see no way out. One day, our 17-year marriage ends. I shock myself as the words escape my lips, "I want a divorce." There is an odd sense of relief to be able to put a stop to the emotional, physical and financial abandonment. Living with the pain every day for many years has been unbearable. Perhaps now the healing can begin?

I make sure to check myself that it is not just an outburst of anger. But no, I am done. The cup is full. It is a personal revolution. The revolution of my soul. I know my decision will bring turmoil and stress. I ask myself if I am up for it. The fear of handling life alone in a country without family, friends, or financial support is terrifying.

I spend time in the darkness of my soul unable to see how I will be happy again. And I am angry; not only with myself and my husband but with those at church who kept telling me I am making a mistake. That he is a good father. He works and takes care of the house and the kids and me. I don't have to worry about finances and a roof over my head. Most couples stop having intimacy over the years, they say to me. It is normal. These talks just trap me in the same shoe I have been wearing for years. It seems that every day, my heart shrinks. For two years I remain in flight or fight mode.

My divorce is uncomplicated. I am free of the unfulfilled expectations that someone would love me for being me. Reflecting back on that time I learnt the most important lesson: I learned to love myself.

Being alone in that darkness brought me back to the depth of my heart where I connected me to my soul both on a physical and spiritual level. A level I had never experienced before. I found out where God lives. I found out where I came from. I found out who I am.

From being scared and angry, I returned home. And that home has everything. Love, connection, understanding, and a place to grow and expand. A place where I never feel abandoned. How did this happen you may ask? Oh, I had to go through another three years of learning. When I thought I was ready to open up to love again, I experienced betrayal and heartbreak once again. That is when I let it all go; the hopes and trials, pain and lies.

This experience did not make me thick-skinned; instead, it gave me an opportunity to return to my childhood wound and once again meet that baby girl, who was still looking for a connection to be protected, cared for, and loved. And that girl met me. She became a friend. I provided understanding, love, and care. She knows her worth because she is always loved. She is loved by me. I know her better than anyone else. Every need and every desire. She doesn't have to expect to be loved and accepted any longer. I accept her. She is never abandoned. And never will be.

I had learned that the only way out is finding the way in. They say that after a divorce you get a new start, but I say it's an expansion beyond. But first I had to return to my true self; the self that got lost in the shuffle of life.

One day, I called a friend and asked her for any book recommendations she might have on how to begin restoring myself. She responded, "Do this every day. I don't care how many times you can do it, just do it. Look in the mirror deep into your eyes and say: I am sorry. Forgive me. I love you. Thank you."

That morning I drop my kids at school and return home, I walk into the bathroom, close the door and I look into the mirror, and say, "I am sorry. Forgive me. I love you. Thank you."

Tears roll down my cheeks. I can't see my reflection any longer. I see my soul looking into my eyes. A soul that is beautiful and has only love for me. There is no fear; only love, compassion and understanding. I see my soul with my own eyes. My heart opens and bursts into radiant pure light of joy and happiness.

Never in my life had I experienced such a feeling.
And that was only the beginning. Little by little information started coming into my life. I started listening to high-frequency music that put me into a peaceful state; one that I had never consciously experienced before. I became more curious about myself as a spiritual creation.

Driving down a scenic road in Massachusetts one day, I look up and say to God that what I know is not enough. I want more. And more I get. From the moment I had first felt the merging of my higher spiritual self into my body, there was no point of return to the old me. It was a true bliss.

Over the next four years I learned how to see human and nature's auras. Through shamanic knowledge I understand all my previous supernatural experiences and I find a language for them.

Things start to make sense. I am as surprised as everyone else when a friend comes to me to ask to share my egg with her so she can conceive, only to return home that day and become pregnant from her husband, leaving her doctors in shock. All of these occurrences had an explanation when I learned metaphysics, energies, and the mind. I stopped going to church only to reconnect with God on a new and much deeper level.

I had learned how to heal through sound and how to summon the universal energies within my body and conduct a healing. I became a vessel. I became a healer. I am reminded that life begins with the formation of the heart first. And life has to continue through the heart.

I had learned who I am as a female. I became powerful and more beautiful in my knowledge regarding my own femininity.

The Gift

Life is still challenging but I have created a beautiful harmony within that supports me through everyday living. First, I recognise that fear is self-inflicted. I stop imagining a scary future and instead I focus on the tasks at hand. Work responsibilities remind me that I am able to respond to challenges with my own abilities to process all information and to go with the flow of dealing with each of them. I start my morning by checking in with my heart to see if it has any traces of fear. If there is something uncomfortable, I remind myself that fear is a made-up story. So, I make up a better one. I release it and fill it in with love, grace, and ease. I connect to nature every day. It grounds me in my own energy.

I know I am cared for by a higher power. While I was searching for a place to rent after my divorce, I couldn't picture the beautiful house where my kids and I would end up spending three years. It was a God sent moment as two other families had applied ahead of me. Miraculously, we were the ones to move in. Later on, unable to rent a house without a cosigner I managed to buy the house where we now live and where we are happy.

I have no regrets or lingering pain regarding my path in life. I am happy I have grown into my soul, and it is an experience I wish for all to go through because it is the discovery of true love and connection to the real God who is the creator of all. Who is all.

I started my own business to help others return to the harmonic self. And that's why I named my business "The Return". Through my work I have found friends all over the world. I never feel alone even when I spend my holidays by myself.

The return to myself opened up a new life and a new vision for me on life, death and God. I had learned that Universe is big, and we are not small. We are a part of it.

Healing happens on a personal level. It starts with your decision to heal your heart and transmute all the hurt of your personal experiences into harmony and the knowledge of love.

After returning to myself there is no point of returning back to the life I once knew.

Dr Ashley Ghose

Dr. Ashley Ghose is a physical therapist who has become an Empowerment Mentor. Dr. Ashley realised her patient's where most successful when they benefitted from her combined physical therapist skills and her knowledge on empowerment.
Dr. Ashley has years of experience in helping women with practical solutions to create a stress-free life, improve work life balance and improve mental and physical wellbeing. Find her at www.ashleymghose.com

"It is time to return to who you are and create the habit of being you"
– Dr. Ashley Ghose

Waves of change bring a sea of transformation

It's happening again. I've been here before.
This time it feels different. I don't know what to do.
I have so many thoughts racing through my head as I drag myself up the staircase to change out of my work clothes. With each step my body aches, my jaw is clenched, my shoulders tight, my hands feel like claws, and I feel bone-weary tired.
My thoughts tell me on repeat:

You're not good enough! If you were a better physical therapist you would have enough time to treat your patient's and document their care.

If you were a better mother you would be home on time to help with dinner.

If you were a better wife you would make it a priority to go out to dinner with your husband.

If you were smarter you would not be in this situation.

Small tears well up in my eyes, taking their time to fall slowly but before I know it, I am silently sobbing. My head is in my hands as I sit down heavily on the edge of my bed. Through my wet fingers I can see the blurry blue of my pillowy comforter and the yellow light of the hallway reflected on the carpet underfoot.

Suddenly I am sobbing so hard I nearly lose my seat on the edge of the bed. As my shoulders shake uncontrollably, I raise my eyes to the ceiling.
I can feel my mascara tracking its way down my cheeks, to overtake my runny nose. I don't care. I just sit there.
I drop my gaze again to stare down at my black trousers and red polo shirt; the traditional work attire of a physical therapist as the tears begin to drip off my jaw, they make the fabric of my trousers darker.
What was I going to do? I am a problem solver, a solution finder…
I know, I'll just quit my job and go work at another clinic.
No, that's not good idea, there will be other issues at that clinic.
The grass is not greener on the other side. Come on come up with a

110

real solution, I beg myself. Sarcastically I think, *I know, I will just sit here and cry and that will fix all my problems. What? All my problems? How many problems do I have?*
Oh, my goodness I am so messed up...so broken...
I start to sob silently again, my head back in my hands. I don't want anyone downstairs to know I am upset; I'm embarrassed to be upset. I don't want to be here crying my eyes out, I want to be downstairs with my kids and husband laughing at the television show with them as the characters of the show do funny things.
I don't want to think about work or how bad of a therapist, mother, and wife I am.
The sobbing slows.
I start to think of the other times in my life I felt this way. I am not sure if I am looking for solutions or looking for evidence to justify my sobbing.
Memories came flooding back, like waves of a strong tide washing in. The first wave hits.
I'm in elementary school. I don't fit the mold of the typical, average student; I don't feel understood. I love to learn yet the more schooling I do, the more difficulty I am having. At the suggestion of a teacher, my parents decide to have me tested for a learning disability. We do this outside of the school system since my mother doesn't want the school system to label me.

I remember that warm Fall day, and the cold classroom chair against the back of my bare knees, as I get ready to hear my test results alongside my mom in the testing center. The examiner slides the paper in front of my mother and I, across the white table and begins to talk. I hear concern in her voice, "Ashley is at or below grade level for reading, spelling, and math. While she is well above grade level in other areas, I don't know why she is having trouble in her academics at school." I am bitterly disappointed; I had hoped we would find a way to fix me. I want to stop feeling so sad, so desolate and disappointed at getting only one word correct on my spelling tests after so much studying. I notice the look on my classmates' faces which speaks louder than words. "You only got one word correct?" they chime as they display their perfect scores.

My parents find a solution; I have a tutor for a few years which really helps however, at the time we were unaware that I had dyslexia.

It would be another few years before we discovered that there are many types of dyslexia. All I knew is that I had to endure hours of studying to keep up; school was a momentous effort fuelled by my drive and commitment not to disappoint myself and everyone else.

Then the second wave.

It's a pleasant memory the day I discovered dance and how it l changed my life. I had found a way to express myself without the need to write or read things correctly. A year after I start dancing however, I develop knee pain. No physician I saw knew how to help my knee pain. My only solutions were to stop dancing or dance with knee braces. Imagine telling a 15-year-old to stop doing the thing they love? There was no way that was happening. This was time I didn't fit the mold of an injured athlete. I decide to start educating the physician about dance. When I was injured the second time I still felt misunderstood regarding the pain now in my back..
 I decide then and there to become someone that could help dancers feel understood during their injuries.
I smoothed the wrinkles of the plush comforter; I was feeling a little more empowered. My crying had faltered to a stop but still no solution…
    The third wave was at college.
I wanted my passion for dance to be my career and my parents wanted me to go to college. The easy solution was for me to go to college to study dance. Since my parents didn't want me to end up as a starving artist, they insisted I choose a back up career in addition to dance. After many discussions, including some of the loud variety, I attended college to study dance medicine. Not only would I have something to fall back on, but I would also be going into healthcare. At least for my own personal fulfilment I was doing something I loved and filling the requirements of my concerned parents.
I really enjoyed college, yet once again I didn't feel like I really fitted in. I was one of two people who were double majoring in Dance and Science. My dancer friends didn't understand the world of Science and versa. This left me in the middle, not sure which side to embrace, creativity or logic.
I started to be what people wanted me to be.

In the dance world I was a dancer, creative and fun. In the world of science, I was logical and nerdy. I had discovered a new version of Dr Jekyll and Mrs. Hyde.

The fourth wave finds me in Graduate school.

I decided I wanted to help dancers via physical therapy. I could finally be the person who helped dancers recover from their injuries and even prevent injuries! The fast pace and high demands of physical therapy school took their toll.

My fear was real and present when our anatomy teacher told the class half our grade would be based on spelling the body's anatomy correctly.

I thought, you've got to be kidding me, I can barely spell the word anatomy.

The slow tears well back up again at the sharp memory. *Why I am I so messed up? Is it helping me to think of these events? Is there a key to discovering how to move forward?*

I take a deep breath. I feel my ribcage expand in a hiccup, the tears tracking their way down my cheeks. This memory reminds me of how far I have traveled away from myself and my true passion. Once out in the working world, I had yearned to be a team player and please my boss, so I became a specialist in an area that was not dance. I saw how messed up it was, putting someone else's wants and needs before my own.

What am I going to do?

I take another breath; the tears have stopped for now.

Just then, I hear a divine voice in my head, "you are not here on earth to live a miserable life." My mind is quick to retort, *Yeah, right? Did you not see all the times in my life, including this one, that my brokenness has left me in a situation where there is no solution?*

I take another breath. I think about the words a little more, 'you are not here on earth to live a miserable life'. Could that statement be true? The answer I receive is the sound of a loud belly laugh coming from my son, daughter and husband which rises up the staircase from their position in front of the television show.

This is my answer, laughter, the truest form of laughter, the laughter that causes you to fight for air to breath, causes your stomach to hurt. This is it! I can live a life that is meaningful and be happy at the same time.

I wipe the tears from my face and quickly change so I can become a part of the joy that is happening downstairs.

Later, I reluctantly share everything with my husband. That night we have a wonderful conversation. More tears come, as well as solutions. As we talk, I can see my way through to my first steps.

My first adjustment is to bring creativity back into my life.

It's the first of many small adjustments that allowed me to heal my trauma of overwhelm and transform into the grounded, joyful and peace-filled person I am today.

Lessons Learnt

It became clear that I have spent much of my life working to fit into a mold, an idea of the person I was supposed to be in the world. I believed I could not be myself since I was broken, dyslexic and too unique. I was suffering from the dichotomy of being equally creative and logical so no one could relate to me; I was too different.

Looking back, I discovered a new pattern of awareness, together with forgiveness for the people I had held responsible for causing me to create these beliefs about myself. But most importantly, I learnt how to forgive myself as the first small steps towards my transformation.

Today, after leaving healthcare to pursue my passion, I can help others understand they are not alone. Most importantly that they can heal from chaos and overwhelm, and that perfection is not the solution. I thought I was broken because of my dyslexia but now I know it allows me to see the world in a unique way. Through daily habits I am rewiring my brain from being a hyper-focused perfectionist to a high achiever who is fully embracing myself and who I truly am.

I find so much joy in supporting my clients in the journey of self-discovery for themselves.

In Unlock Keys to Understanding You, you will learn, the 4 keys steps to breaking out of exhaustion and overwhelm to find clarity to discovering your true authentic self, create deeper connections in your relationship, support other by becoming a light in the world, and connecting you to your purpose! Download it for free here: https:// bit.ly/UnlockingYouGift

Alena Gomes Rodrigue

Alena Gomes Rodrigue is a trauma-informed mental fitness coach,
former corporate Human Resources leader,
and a proud mom and wife.
Living and working abroad since 2002 and becoming a Mom in 2017,
Alena is passionate about helping professional expat Moms to thrive
abroad. Currently based in Paris, Alena works with English-speaking
women all around the world. Alena is an avid fan of Montessori
education, a humble student of Ashtanga yoga, and a chai tea addict.
https://alenagomesrodrigues.com/

"Someone I loved once gave me a box full of darkness.
It took me years to understand that this too, was a gift."
~ Pema Chödrön

Zen and the Art of Parenting

A grey sky, leaden and heavy hangs over the bustling activity of Prague airport as I wait curb-side for my taxi. I've just landed back on home soil and my stomach is a coil of knots. My phone rings. I reach into my pocket and retrieve it, to see my Dad's name on the screen. My heart stops.

This could mean only one thing…

My suitcase is standing to attention at my feet, neatly packed with my black funeral wear. I had taken off three weeks from my corporate job in Belgium so that I could spend the last moments with my Mom in the hospital. The doctors were not giving her any more time than that.

I remember the day Mom told me she was sick. We were standing in my kitchen, I was making her a cup of tea, she had just returned from her hospital appointment to see what the lump in her breast was.

As I stir the tea, I am listening to her every word but it seems as if someone has turned time to slow-motion. I stop stirring and stare at the shiny white surface of my kitchen cupboards for what seemed like forever before I finally turned to her.

"You have breast cancer?!"

We embrace, our heads on each other's shoulders, as silent tears roll down my face, blurring my vision, and it strikes me that we have never done this before.

Could it really have been just three years since I had seen her suffer through and recover from this cancer? It had been the darkest time of my life and it was only in the Summer, when she started to get better, that I had applied for my first internship abroad. As I had boarded the plane, I had carried with me a sense of guilt at leaving her but everyone had been optimistic, mom was fighting it like the lioness she was.

After a year of hope and remission, however, cancer had returned. It was back, bigger and stronger than before, attacking her digestive system and her spine.

And I had not been there for her this time to support her recovery.

Living and working in Belgium, I would fly home for a week out of each month to visit Mom. It didn't feel enough, and yet, I'm ashamed to admit, I was secretly happy that I was able to depart each time, to return to my life abroad where I didn't have to see Mom suffer such terrible pain, her body getting weaker and more fragile each day.

I tried to hold on to the image of my Mom as the powerful, energetic woman who could always beat any odds. A memory flashes back of her marching in her high heels through the halls of the most prestigious Bakery in the region where she is the only female Chief Financial Officer and Member of the Board. My Mom could run the world with her charisma and strength.

I finally pick up the call.

- *Dad?*

- *Alenko, the hospital just called, she's gone. Come straight home, there's no need to go to the hospital anymore.*

I nearly drop the phone as tears burst forth, a waterfall of salty grief. I don't try to stop them and I don't care about the stares I'm getting as I stand alone on the curb. *I didn't make it on time, SHAME ON ME!*

I was NOT there AGAIN.

And now it's too late.

I watch the landscape pass silently by, behind the taxi's side window. I'm slowly calming down. Well, at least my mom is not in pain anymore.

But, this is it for me now.

My Grandma got breast cancer when she was in her 40's, and my Mom as well, so it's my turn now. I'm 27, does that mean I have only a few more years to go?

I don't want to die at 51 like my mom! Heck, I want to live till 100 at least!

No freaking way!

This will NOT happen to me!

The Missing Link

The next couple of months and years were frustrating. I felt I was doing all I could to live a healthy life: limiting sugar, fat, fried and processed food, working out four to six times a week, I never smoked, but it didn't seem enough.

How can I prevent cancer from attacking my body?

My days were fuelled with constant fear. Every time I saw someone smoking I would silently ask 'why are you killing yourself'. I didn't feel safe. My thoughts would turn to my numbered years; I'm still single, I have no kids, my time is running out. At age thirty-two, it wasn't just my biological clock but my Cancer clock was ticking too.

One day, almost five years after Mom's passing, I was searching online when a new speaker showed up on my feed. It was Dr. Gabor Mate speaking about *"When the Body Says No"*. I got his key message: It's the stress that kills! Stress is the trigger for not only most autoimmune diseases but also for Cancer.

Hearing Dr. Mate talk, bits and pieces of childhood memories started flash backing in my brain.

It's a few weeks before Christmas. It's already dark outside and the aromas of Cinnamon and Gingerbread spices fill the air. My younger brother and I are stirring and sticking our little pre-schooler fingers into the mix of honey, milk, and flour, doing our best to turn it into a yummy dough for Christmas cookies. Our laughter and excitement are abruptly cut short by Mom's loud, sharp NO!

"What are you kids doing? Look at this mess! And stop eating the dough! The next batch of cookies needs to go in the oven, and it can't look like THIS, what would people say? I'll be here all night if you keep slowing me down! Get out of my way!

I look at Mom and see her witch-like face. It is scrunched up and tight with anger and tiredness. I quickly get out of her way.

Mom always had so much to do. I didn't enjoy Christmas or any other large family events because it always meant more work for her. This made me anxious. I knew she was inevitably going to get angry and stressed, and we'd all be walking around on eggshells, careful not to become her target.

And then, as if you had waved a magic wand, Mom put on her 'perfect hostess' face and the event was ready to begin.
Alright then, so it was super-stress that killed my super-Mom through cancer…

Sitting on the terrace of my penthouse, I gaze up at the tip of the Eiffel Tower in the distance, and it hits me…
But I've been heading in the same direction!

In a rare moment of contemplation, I turn my gaze towards the bedroom, and there they were. All my 'trophies' of achievement and success. My certificates are displayed on the wall; together with the long lines of postcards that I bought in all the places where I lived, worked, and traveled. Below the windowsill, my bookshelf is filled with volumes on coaching, leadership and personal growth. And of course, I couldn't miss it; there was my shoe rack displaying all my pairs of high-heeled shoes.

I've come a long way for a shy Czech girl from a little mountain village. Mom would have been proud.

BUT…

As my business mentor, Luc, had commented during our first session, it was obvious how much time and energy I devoted to work and my self-development. He gently suggests "Maybe you could stop planning even your weekends by the hour and schedule in some *un*scheduled time for a breather, just to have fun?"

My brain starts to unravel this information from a new angle. As if it's a movie running backward, I start to see the pattern of my life. It becomes clear I have been running in the same direction as my Mom, stressed, overworked, with no downtime.

I want to prove I'm not only good enough, but that I'm the best I can be, so no one can say I'm just another Eastern European girl looking for a rich husband in the West. To prove I'm worthy of love, my work results must be perfect, I don't want to upset anyone because they expected more from me, like that Christmas evening baking Christmas cookies so long ago.

At the time, I took Luc's comment as a compliment. It was my badge of honor, and I was proud of my discipline. After all, I wanted to be like my mom, competent successful, perfect and always on time! Until now.

I get it. The risk I'm running is clear. If I keep pushing hard and being overworked, exhausted, and stressed, I will likely end up with Cancer like Mom. The very thing I am running away from, I am running towards.

But what is the alternative?!

The Tipping Point

* * *

Sunlight is streaming through the bedroom windows, but I barely notice. I'm dressing my daughter and Ella's two-year-old arms still needed help finding their way inside the sleeves of her jacket. Today, she's even more excited and playful than usual, hiding her arm and escaping my repeated attempts to get her ready to leave for the park.

I notice the critical voice inside my head which never stops. *You've got so much to do after you come back, let's not waste any more time with this nonsense. Let's go!*

"STOP!" I finally yell at the playful Ella. I see the laughter wiped from her face, only to be replaced with surprise, which quickly turns into wide-eyed fear.

I see my witch face reflected in Ella's eyes, and I am transported back to the Christmas evening baking cookies in the kitchen.
I have become my Mom, witch face included!

Now it's my turn to be surprised." I'm so sorry," I tell Ella as I comfort her. But a small part of me still wants that time for what I love doing: my coaching practice, reading, exercising. Is it too much to ask for?
How can I do it all and be a loving Mom without taking on the stress, anger, and resentment I saw so vividly reflected in my Mother?

Getting to the roots of trauma

I made it my mission in the next few days to not overbook my schedule and keep some time for myself. One evening I even managed to take a warm bath with lavender and chamomile to relax. *Victory!*

And yet, I found myself lying there, still frowning and tight, with the long to-do list running through my head. I noticed that voice in my head again…

This is what lazy people do! You're wasting your precious time here and there's so much to get done! Get out quickly!

I realized that voice was never happy no matter how much I tried, how well I did. It was always pushing me to do more.

And the worst was, I couldn't turn it off!
Can you get rid of the voices in your head?

I wanted to turn off my inner critic in my head, but I was also grateful for how it pushed me to achieve everything I have ever

120

wanted, including a corporate career abroad, the switch to building my own business and creating a coaching practice. I didn't want to get rid of it completely, I just wanted to be able to control it so that it would let me de-stress, so I could stop shouting at my daughter and not die of cancer like my Mom.

But I had no idea how to do that or where to go.

I love coaching but it doesn't stop the past from popping up. And therapy is for traumatised people. I had had a happy childhood overall. I didn't want to spend years talking about my Mom and blaming her for everything. I loved her!

And then I came across the work of Lion Goodman, the founder of Clear Beliefs Institute. He trains coaches to clear and heal deep-seated patterns and belief systems. Knowing how much I struggled with my own beliefs about Supermoms, over-achievers and perfectionism, I wanted to give it a try.

Little did I know it was to become the key to my redemption and the cornerstone of how I help my clients.

Subconscious Mind Surgery: Getting to the Core

It's a warm summer afternoon with a light breeze. I'm helping mom hang the laundry on the line. I feel so proud that I can help her save some time!

I'm 4 and I'm a big girl, like my mom!

I will make her smile and then she'll play with me.

But instead, Mom comments, "You're doing it the same wrong way as your father does. You're little, it's ok. But he should have known better." And she starts taking off the cloth pegs that I have placed on the socks and underwear and turns them all in a different direction.

In an instant, my pride turns to shame and disappointment.

That's one of my first memories that I 'unearthed' during the Clear Beliefs training. It's silly from an adult perspective, nothing really happened, right?

That was the moment I realised *I was not good enough.*

I have to try harder to make my Mom happy.

And I must be perfect, otherwise it doesn't count.

This is the first step of the mind 'surgery' process I learned from Lion Goodman – discovering what the roots of our beliefs are about.

Not only what happened, but more importantly, *what you made it mean about yourself.* What belief you accepted as truth, and how you looked at your life through its' lens ever since.

There's something wrong with me, I'm not good enough the way I am.

I'm not worthy of love.

If only I try hard enough and achieve enough, I will be loved and appreciated.

Once you know what the real cause is, you can start healing it.

Healing the Childhood Wounds: Belief Closet Process

Have you ever gone in search of the core of your stress?

Have you identified that moment in your childhood when you realised (or to be precise, someone made you aware) that you were not good enough and had to strive for perfection to be worthy of love and appreciation?

Is that the belief you accepted as a truth about yourself?

And would you like to let go of it once and for all?

Let me walk you through a simple version of the process I use in my coaching practice with my clients who battle with the challenge of wanting to do it all.

Proceed slowly through the following steps, allow space for your subconscious mind to process it.

Focus on the belief that you identified as core.

Feel what it feels like to have that belief, fully in your body.

Once you got it, imagine that feeling is an outfit, a piece of clothing you could put on.

What does it look like?

How does it feel wearing it?

Does it have any smell or make any sound?

Now that you see it's the outfit producing all those feelings, take it off.

Just take it off, put it on the floor and notice all the feelings that came off with it. Because it was the outfit that was producing them.

Once you took it all off, are you ready to let it go?

You can go ahead and burn it in your mind, if you'd like.

If you feel resistance towards burning it, there might be several things going on.

This belief and outfit might have protected you in the past. What was it protecting you from?

Another possibility is that this belief was never yours in the first place, and so it's not yours to burn.

This was my case. The belief *I need to prove I'm worthy of love and appreciation by working as hard as I can* was never mine to start with. It was my Mom's belief about herself, and she made me feel the same way about me.

Give Back Ceremony:

If you know who gave you that belief, you can choose to give it back to them in your imagination.

That's how I gave back my 'perfectionist achiever' armour to my mom and together we decided to burn it, not only on our behalf, but in the name of all women in our lineage who just wanted to be seen, understood, and loved unconditionally.

Because it was not just Cancer being passed down the lineage, it was also that perfectionist overachiever's burden. We all felt we had to prove being worthy of love and appreciation.

And I was able to forgive my Mom for being too busy to love me. For wanting me to be a perfect cookie cutter version of herself.

If you feel exhausted every minute of the day and your critical voice is beating you up and constantly pushing you to do and achieve more, please stop.

The answer is not in better productivity techniques, more self-care or mindfulness time, nor it is about choosing between having a career or being a Mom because you can't have it all.

Those are all just symptoms, the tip of that proverbial iceberg.

Thanks to Goodman's techniques, the women I work with heal so much of their past after just few sessions. And imagine what's possible if you keep clearing and healing all your triggers as they come up?

I'm not a 100% Zen supermom 100% of the time. And that's okay. Accepting that I'm perfectly imperfect, and worthy of love just *because I am, not because of what I do*, is all part of the journey. And that's my wish for you.

You can heal.

You can love yourself, your family, and your life, perfectly imperfect.

You can be the Zen supermom, or superdad.

I invite you to dive deeper into some of the beliefs you might be holding onto with a free copy of my Beliefs Journal here **https://alena.clickfunnels.com/beliefsjournal**

Marci Shimoff

— Marci Shimoff is a #1 New York Times bestselling author, a world-renowned transformational teacher and an expert on happiness, success, and unconditional love.

Her books include the international bestsellers Happy for No Reason and Love for No Reason. Marci is also the woman's face of the biggest self-help book phenomenon in history, as co-author of six books in the Chicken Soup for the Woman's Soul series.

With total book sales of more than 16 million copies worldwide in 33 languages, Marci is one of the bestselling female nonfiction authors of all time. Marci is also a featured teacher in the international film and book sensation, *The Secret* and the host of the PBS TV show called Happy for No Reason. She narrated the award-winning movie called Happy.

Marci delivers keynote addresses and seminars on happiness, success, empowerment, and unconditional love to Fortune 500 companies, professional and non-profit organisations, women's associations and audiences around the world. Marci is currently leading a one-year mentoring program called Your Year of Miracles. Her opening seminar has been heard my more than 200,000 people. Marci earned her MBA from UCLA and holds an advanced certificate as a stress management consultant. She is a founding member and on the board of directors of the Transformational Leadership Council, a group of 100 top transformational leaders. Through her books and her presentations, Marci's message has touched the hearts and rekindled the spirits of millions of people throughout the world. She is dedicated to helping people live more empowered and joy-filled lives.

"If there is light in the soul, there will be beauty in the person.
If there is beauty in the person, there will be harmony in the house.
If there is harmony in the house, there will be order in the nation.
If there is order in the nation, there will be peace in the world."
~ Chinese proverb

Becoming Happy for No Reason

What is happiness? It's been my life's work to find the answer to this question. And after years of deep investigation, I have a definition of happiness that's a little different than most -- I call it being "happy for no reason." It doesn't mean walking around with a permanent grin on your face in some Pollyanna state of denial. "Happy for no reason" is about having an inner state of peace and wellbeing that doesn't depend on your outer circumstances.

Instead of trying to extract your happiness from life, you can create an internal state of happiness within that you bring to your life experience.

On a global level, we're facing enormous challenges. And life can throw big challenges at us on a personal level too. When we have an inner foundation of happiness and peace, we are resilient and creative in the face of adversity and can bounce back from challenges more quickly. It's important that we develop a deeper state of unconditional happiness, especially during these times on the planet.

My Story

I was born depressed. I came out of the womb with existential angst. While I had a great family and circumstances, right from the start, I felt a deep heaviness around me. At five years old, I remember being very empathic. My friends would be out playing and laughing, and I would wonder, "How can I be happy when there's so much suffering in the world?".

In order to cope in my childhood and teen years, my solution to my unhappiness was sugar. I became a sugar addict because it was the only thing that made me feel a little better even if only temporarily. By the time I was in high school, I was 35 to 40 pounds overweight. By then I realised that sugar only made me unhappier.

So, in my early 20s, I did what most people do: I set goals for myself. I figured that when I achieved those goals, I would definitely be happy.

I had five goals. I wanted to have a successful career helping people, a wonderful husband or life partner, fabulous friends, a comfortable home, and the equivalent of Halle Berry's body. (I got four out of the five — I don't have Halle Berry's body, but I do have a healthy body for which I'm very grateful.)

I had worked really hard to achieve my major goals in life–and I did. Then, in 1998, I had a turning point moment. I was in Chicago celebrating that I had three books in the top five on the *New York Times* bestseller list, and I'd just finished giving a speech to 8,000 people. After the talk, I had lines around the entire stadium to sign my books. I ended up autographing 5,432 books (my client had a therapist massage my hand so I could keep on signing!).

On the one hand, I felt like an author rock star. When I went up to my hotel room after signing the last book and walked over to the big windows overlooking Lake Michigan, I should have felt on top of the world. But instead, I turned around, collapsed onto the bed, and burst into tears.

I burst into tears because I'd done everything I thought I needed to do to be happy, yet I still felt that emptiness inside. I could no longer fool myself into thinking that the next achievement was going to do it. (We've all had the experience of thinking that when "that thing" happens, then I'll be happy. And then "it" happens, and you're happy for a short period, but then the feeling goes away.)

I said, "I've got to figure this out," and I decided to dive deeply into the study of happiness.

And that kicked off an incredible journey for me. I interviewed one hundred unconditionally happy people (who I called the "Happy 100") and all the experts on happiness I could find. I started doing what they were telling me, and… it really worked!

If you were giving me a grade, I would say that I went from a D+ in the subject of happiness to an A! I'm still a work in progress, but I'm a solid A.

I was so excited about what I discovered that I decided to write a book called *Happy for No Reason*. I've now taught the methods in this book to hundreds of thousands of people in talks around the world, and millions of people around the world have bought my books.

Now, I know for sure that you can become happier no matter what --, whether you're really unhappy right now or already very happy.

My friend Lisa Nichols says, "Our mess becomes our message." I love this phrase... I believe that, had I been born happy, I wouldn't be doing this work. So, my unhappiness ultimately had a higher purpose. Whatever you're going through, ask: "If this were happening for a higher purpose, what might that be?"

Cracking the Happiness Code: Your Happiness Setpoint

I have good news and bad news for you about happiness. The bad news is that humans have more than we've ever had before on a material level, and yet we're suffering from an epidemic of unhappiness and depression. So, happiness is not about "things." The good news is that science has cracked the happiness code and there's the science about how to be happy! Now, this should be headline news and taught in every school!

What I discovered in my research is that we all have something called a happiness set-point—it's like a thermostat setting. Whether good or bad, no matter what happens to us, we'll return to our happiness set-point unless we consciously do something to change it. For example, if someone wins the lottery, it doesn't always lead to greater happiness. It may help for a couple of months, but studies show that even after winning the lottery, people will generally return to their original happiness set-point within about a year. This set-point or thermostat setting is the key to our happiness, and anybody can change their happiness set-point.

Your happiness set-point is 50% genetic, you're born with it. (I was not born with the happy genes.) Now here's what's really important: Your happiness set-point is only 10% of your circumstances. Most people are so busy trying to create all the right circumstances in their lives so they can be happy. Maybe they had the thought, "Oh, I'll focus on getting everything in the right place, and then I'll be happy." Forget it; it's not going to work—your circumstances account for only 10% of your happiness set-point.

The other 40% of your happiness set-point is your habits of thoughts and behavior. And this is where we have the most power to shift our happiness.

I'm going to take it a step further and say that scientists in the field of epigenetics, like Dr. Bruce Lipton, have found that our genes are influenced when we change our habits of thoughts and behavior. This means that 90% of the happiness set-point can be influenced by changing our thoughts and behavior!

So, even if we have inherited unhappiness in our genes, we aren't stuck with it. You can do something about your happiness set-point, and it's actually not as hard as you think.

In my extensive research, I found that there are 21 main Happiness Habits that people can practice to raise their set-point and they fall into seven main categories.

Happiness Habits: Building Your Inner Home for Happiness

Every home has seven main components: a foundation, four corner pillars, a roof, and a garden. There are seven categories of the Happiness Habits, each of which I have associated with each component of a home. In this way, you can think about raising your happiness set-point as "building your Inner Home for Happiness."

Taking Responsibility for Your Life

1. The Foundation: The foundation of the home is about taking responsibility for your life and your happiness. That means not showing up as a victim and showing up as a victor or a co-creator in your life instead.

You know you're being a victim when you're doing one of three things: blaming others or blaming your circumstances, complaining about whatever's going on, or shaming, which means self-blame or shaming yourself. So, if you find yourself blaming, shaming, or complaining regularly, you can choose to take more responsibility for your happiness.

The four corner pillars of the house are the mind, the heart, the body, and the soul.

2. The Pillar of the Mind: The mind represents your thoughts: Do your thoughts rob you of your happiness?

3. The Pillar of the Heart: Do you live with an open heart? I've never met a happy person who had a closed heart. Do you live from kindness, love, forgiveness, generosity, and gratitude?

4. The Pillar of the Body: Do you have the biochemistry of happiness? Do you have enough serotonin, oxytocin, dopamine, GABA, endorphins, and happy chemicals? If not, there are ways to increase them.

5. The Pillar of the Soul: The pillar of the soul has to do with your connection to all of life: Do you feel connected to the source of energy in life, whether you call it God, or Spirit, the Divine, creative intelligence, or nature?

6: The Roof: The roof of your home for happiness has to do with your purpose or passion in life: Are you living a passionate life? Are you doing what you're here on this planet to do? Do you wake up inspired?

7: The Garden: The garden of your Inner Home for Happiness has to do with the people that you surround yourself with. Do you have toxic people, like the weeds in your garden, dragging you down? Or do you have roses and gardenias surrounding you? people who are supporting your happiness?

Most of us have one or two areas that are weaker than the others, and they buckle when we're under pressure. When things get a little stressful, we may lose our step somewhere, and that's usually the area where we need to go back and set things right again.

For me, it's the Pillar of the Body. I didn't have the neurochemistry of happiness growing up. These days, if my happiness levels start to drop, I know that's the first place I need to look. I ask myself: Am I getting enough exercise? Am I getting the right supplements? Am I getting enough sleep?

Once you identify which area is your downfall, you know where to start building yourself up to raise your happiness set-point. That's where you're going to get the most noticeable change.

I find that for most people, the weakest area is the Pillar of the Mind. The average person has 60,000 thoughts a day, and 80% of those are negative. It's called the negativity bias—we inherited it from our caveman ancestors, who had to remember the negatives in order to stay alive. Happier people have created new neural pathways in their brains for the positive rather than the negative. My dear friend, Rick Hansen, calls it the Velcro /Teflon syndrome. He says, "Our minds are like Velcro for the negative—they just stick to us—but like Teflon for the positive; the positive slides off." Happy people have reversed that. They have the positive stick, and the negative slide off.

3 Ways to Start Creating New Neural Pathways of Happiness
There are three simple things you can do to start creating new neural pathways so that the positives stick more.

1. Be on the lookout for the positive.
We need to actively train our minds to be on the lookout for the positive. One of the women I interviewed for *Happy For No Reason* pretends that she's on the Academy Awards committee, and her job every day is to give out five Academy Awards. In this way, she's always on the lookout for the positive. If she sees somebody doing a kind act, that person gets the "Kindest Act of the Day" Award. If she sees an adorable fluffy little white dog walking in the park, the dog gets the "Cutest Dog of the Day" Award. Be on the lookout for five positive things a day, and if you have children, play this game with them.

2. Savour the positive for at least 20 seconds.
It's not enough to just experience something positive — we have to let it sink deeply into our body and into our cells in order for the experience to create enough of an impression to create new neural pathways in the brain. That means if you're looking at a beautiful sunset, you don't just say, "Oh, that's a pretty sunset," and walk away. You stand there for 20 seconds, fully enjoying it, like taking a bite of delicious food, and allowing it to register in your body.

3. Go for a 3:1 ratio: three positives to every one negative.
When the negatives show up and you notice them, look for three positives for every one negative. This helps train your mind to always

be looking for the positive.

Practice these three steps for a couple of weeks, and you'll start developing new neural pathways in your brain where things will automatically get better in your life. I've found that people can start to raise their happiness set-point more quickly and easily than they think. It's a matter of getting started and taking a little baby step every day. It's not about doing it all at once. Just take five minutes a day; a couple of minutes here, a couple of minutes there — that's it! because it's a matter of practicing these habits that will create the change. I've observed that when people take on some happiness practices, within about a month, they start feeling different.

Is It Selfish to Want to Be Happy?

People often ask me, "Marci, is it selfish to want to be happy?" My answer is that it is the least selfish thing you could possibly do because when you become happier, you raise your happiness set-point, and it affects everybody around you. Ultimately, it's one thing that each of us can do to help contribute to this planet of ours.

There's a beautiful Chinese proverb that goes: "When there is light in the soul, there will be beauty in the person. When there is beauty in the person, there will be harmony in the house. When there is harmony in the house, there will be order in the nation. And when there is order in the nation, there will be peace in the world."

My wish for every one of us is that we know that light in our own souls, and experience a deeper state of happiness, and through that, we help create more peace on this planet of ours.

Would you like to dive deeper into all of the Happiness Habits?
You can receive a gift from me of all 21 of the Happiness Habits plus a practice to go along with each of them and an assessment of where you are on the happiness scale. It's all on my website at: www.happyfornoreason.com. I also help people around the world live in what I call the "Miracle Zone" through my programs Your Year of Miracles and a Month of Money Miracles. Learn more at www.youryearofmiracles.com.

Sabine Thomas

Sabine Thomas is a practical, empowering Energy Healer and Teacher. She shares her transformational healing knowledge through her *Art of Healing* sessions, workshops and interpersonal training to awaken your innate wisdom so you may claim your birthright to health every day. She continues to share free energy healing sessions with the global community three times a week over Zoom. Experience the power of energy healing when you connect at http//:www.sabinethomas.com

"Energy is the basic ingredient of the universe, and it is readily available for anyone to tap into and draw from its infinite supply. Let me show you how."
– Sabine Thomas, Art of Healing

Journey from the Brink: Learning to Heal

My personal journey, which led me to the Art of Healing, is a miraculous story which almost claimed my life in tropical Africa. I share it with you here, so that you too may come to realize that anything in life is possible.

It all began more than 35 years ago with my first job. At just 18 years old I found my dream job working for a French non-governmental organisation (NGO) which managed an airline service providing competitive airline tickets into Africa. In return for reduced rates, philanthropical passengers would travel to do humanitarian work within the region. This could include the building of schools, planting of vegetable gardens, medical services or teaching skills to communities. As a young girl having grown up in a small village in France, I loved the freedom and opportunity it gave me to travel to Africa and experience new places. I was put in charge of flights to Burkina Faso, and I embraced every opportunity it gave me to explore; firstly, it is the capital city of Ouagadougou, and then onto it's neighbouring countries, traversing most of West Africa by plane, bush taxi or train.

One day, however, while visiting Ouagadougou, I began to feel ill. At first, I found it difficult to eat as my body became inflamed and I fought a constant, biting pain all over my body; with my head feeling as if it would burst. I quickly became weak and with my condition so debilitating, I was admitted to the local hospital. Nurses, then doctors, then professors came to see me, and then the Sangoma, a traditional African mystic. Despite many blood tests and examinations, doctors remained perplexed. Since no one knew what was wrong and my condition continued to deteriorate, the consensus was that I needed to fly back home to France as soon as possible.

Arriving home with the diagnosis of having been 'infected with an unknown virus', I was immediately transported to the Centre for Tropical Diseases in Paris.

Wasting Away

By this time I was wasting away. I couldn't eat or drink and lay on the bed, hardly able to move, too weak to think of anything. It got worse and I was placed in quarantine. Doctors were too scared to come near me in case the dreaded virus was contagious. There I was behind a glass partition, cut off from everyone and feeling as if even the doctors had given up. It appeared as if everyone was just waiting for me to die. Eventually, this is the conclusion I came to as well; I was also waiting to die. Once this was determined, I felt a longing to return home to my mother, choosing to rather die with loved ones surrounding me, than in a hospital with strangers, while trapped inside an isolation ward. The hospital was only too happy to see me go. I was the 'hopeless case' they didn't really want to be reminded of; and they released me.

It isn't easy for any mother to watch her child slowly waste away. None of my mother's efforts to feed me worked; I couldn't keep anything down. She was beside herself with worry and distress. It was no use contacting more doctors; we had already seen all the experts.

Mysterious Healer

In our neighbourhood, there was a man renowned for healing sick people. Mother had heard a few stories shared about him but hadn't really paid much attention until now. She introduced the idea to me saying she thought I should give him a chance. Wracked by pain, unable to move and sensing a foreshadowing of death, I said weakly, "Yes, I want to see him." Despite my resignation, there was still hope.

Almost immediately, the man came to the house. He wasn't anyone I had ever seen before. He was in his fifties with fair hair, and he only charged those who could pay. He didn't ask me any questions; I didn't have to fill in any forms and he didn't ask for my doctor's reports or blood tests. All he did was gently place his hands on specific spots along my spine. He didn't press anything or adjust my bones. He took a few intentional breaths and after about five minutes, he left.

I was devastated. Why did he leave? Perhaps, just like the other doctors, he didn't think anything could be done? My glimmer of hope evaporated, and I felt like curling into a ball and crying. I had expected him to do something. Or, at least, thought he would stay longer. But the next day, the healer knocked at the door. He was back! Once again, he placed his hands on my back for two minutes. He kept on coming, once a day, for five minutes at a time. On the fourth day, to my complete amazement, I was hungry. For the first time in weeks, I felt like eating.

Mother's Prayer Answered

This was all mother needed. She cooked up a delicious meal of fresh vegetables and I not only ate it but also kept it down. For the first time since the illness, I had managed to eat. And what's more, my body felt as if life was returning; I could function again. The pain was no longer debilitating, and I felt emotions such as joy returning after each session. We had no idea what this mysterious and magical healer was doing, but whatever it was, it was working. His visits became the highlight of my day.

Another week went by, and I had enough strength to get out of bed on my own. After two weeks life was almost back to normal. I had put on weight and felt incredible. This man, this stranger, had literally saved my life. My illness had gone. When even the most highly qualified physicians and specialists had no idea how to even begin to treat me, this man in his unassuming manner, without any medicines had restored my health in just two weeks. I was not only intrigued, but I also wanted to know everything about his healing method. After bombarding him with hundreds of questions I found out where these life energy healing courses were offered and enlisted in my first workshop. This experience changed the direction of my life.

Devoted to Healing

My experience occurred many years ago, and ever since, I have devoted my life to advancing my own knowledge in the art of healing and transformative energy healing work, traveling the world and learning from a host of amazing world healers and masters. It was a privilege to spend many years in training with a Vietnamese Master, learning from monks in India, visiting Australia to meditate on Uluru, attending Shamanic initiations in Costa Rica and in Africa, and discovering many more modalities through my travels.

Throughout this time, I have also been privileged to meet and learn from incredible human beings like Dr Joe Dispenza, Dr John Demartini, Tony Robbins, Dr Eric Pearl and Dr David Berceli and along the way I was amazed that some of these special healers and masters were considering me as someone with certain knowledge and expertise too; even asking me for healing sessions. It was a surprise for me because they were my guides and teachers. I remember during his workshop, Dr Pearl asked me up on stage to give him an energy healing. When I put my hand on his shoulder, it cracked loudly to the point where the participants could hear it though his microphone, and his shoulder was back to normal again. Astonished, he rewarded me with the most enormous smile on his face.

In India, Australia and Europe, many individuals and experiences have pushed me to develop my own practice. Over all those years, I have been able to advance my latent talent and healing abilities.

My journey brought me to South Africa where I believe there is a strong need for healing, especially healing that doesn't cost anything. The people of Africa have such open hearts and so easily embrace the concepts taught by *Art of Healing.* Here, it seems a natural part of their culture to share life-giving energy and living in Africa gives me so much joy. Every day I appreciate the wonderful scenery, the aliveness of its people, the color, enthusiasm, and passion for life.

Lockdown Challenge

Now, let's fast forward to the start of the pandemic in early 2020. On hearing of the lockdown, my immediate response was to organize a free online transfer of energy over the Zoom app. Since then, we've had more than 28 000 connections coming online for a transfer of energy with amazing results.

It's heart-warming when people come back to me with news that their thyroid is back to normal, or they don't have a specific issue with asthma anymore, or their wife's dementia problems have dramatically improved.

Experiencing such gratitude and happiness supports me to continue to serve our global community during these difficult times and I continue to offer three five-minute online sessions a week, with people tuning in from all over the world to receive a download of vital healing energy. This is supported by my students whom I have trained in the Art of Healing, where not a day goes by without an email or phone call from them with their stories of miraculous healings experienced on themselves and those around them. This is life-giving!

Besides healing illnesses that have absolutely no known cure, the *Art of Healing* is something that can be applied daily to keep us in a state of well-being. It requires only a small time investment each day and delivers such huge benefit that I believe everyone should be offered the right to use it.

Time to Awaken Your Abilities

It is my life mission to awaken your abilities; like mine were. To spread the knowledge of the *Art of Healing* so that everyone can claim their birthright to absolute healing, absolute energy, and absolute joy. You don't need to be spiritually gifted; you just need to follow simple healing guidelines to achieve success.

A unique epoch has arrived in our history. This is an important time to move out of apathy; a time to raise our frequency as high as possible and express our latent abilities, before it's too late and regardless of what is happening around us.

At this moment in our planet's history, our willingness and determination to express our Divine Nature will play a vital role in our evolution. If we change, the world will change. Everyone can have a positive impact on our collective health, with this limitless and magnificent energy.

Sharing the Art of Healing

Inspired by my Vietnamese Master, I share the *Art of Healing* methodology with thousands of students, and they are implementing the method all over the world with amazing results. *Art of Healing* methodology is easy to learn, and it delivers immediate results, with a simple technique that anybody can learn. Whether you believe it, it still works. It is not reliant on a certain diet, medication, surgery, or chanting. It is not subject to restrictions or limitations, and it is not medically prognostic. The techniques can help any illness or condition.

Nobody should have to live in pain, fear, or disease. We can all take personal responsibility for the quality and state of our health, for health is our birthright.

Join me in a celebration and acknowledgment of our innate ability to heal on all levels, to become whole, and to share that healing with others. Join me online and learn how to use the *Art of Healing* and reclaim perfect health for you and all of humanity.

Christy Whitman

Christy Whitman is a Transformational Leader, Celebrity Coach and Law of Attraction expert for the last twenty years, as well as twice New York Times bestselling author of *The Art of Having It All* and *Taming Your Alpha Bitch*. Known as the girl who "has it all" among her peers this was not always the case. Christy was outwardly successful but inwardly trapped, until she decided to make a change…

"My life had no direction and no meaning.
I was just paying the bills and fulfilling my needs and wants.
This is what happiness is supposed to look like, right?
What I wanted – was purpose. But I didn't even know what purpose
felt like.
All I knew was that it didn't feel like this."
~ Christy Whitman

Watch Your Words, Raise Your Energy and Magnetize

I had achieved my dream. I was making money, I had career success, and I had been on a personal growth journey for some time, yet I still did not feel purposeful in what I was doing. It was only when I started feeling the energy of purpose and started cultivating it through meditation that I realised I was finally operating from the energy of fulfilment instead of lack. That is when I started feeling I was coming from a place of purpose, and that is when my first book came through me! The journey of becoming an author and a coach, a healer and a channeller opened for me; before that, I did not even know that this existed.

When we start to feel the energy of something, we are able to draw it to ourselves. Sometimes, things are beyond our conscious awareness; we do not even know they exist as possibilities. There are so many things we do not know of yet, but when we align with them, we can just pull them in. When we allow the mind to let go and stop clutching onto all the details that we think we have to push forth and figure out, when we allow the energy to lead, then we start to manifest.

When you start to connect with the energy of what you actually want to manifest, then you notice where you are not fully embodying it. When you feel connected to your purpose and you feel pulled, but you are not there, it feels like you have split energy. When you try to experience purpose, but you are resisting, then the body may communicate. You may be given a twinge or a pain, or something may manifest in the body so that you have to clear it. This may force you to learn how to work with energy principles in order to learn to command and move energy in your own body.

Even the blocks holding you back are energy: past blocks, traumatic experiences, or moments when something shocked you or you were sideswiped are energy. The energy may be forms of abuse or receiving news that someone you loved passed on; it could be the death of a family dog or a car accident. These surprises are not the delights in life. Those are the times in your energy field when you close down your heart, like a turtle trying to go inside of his shell. When you close down around those emotions, your energy gets stuck, and it creates a block. That energy still needs to spiral and spiral and spiral, so it starts to create a vortex that starts attracting things to you. **When you find you are attracting things to you that you do not want, it is an indication that there's a block somewhere.**

If you want to release the block, it is possible to take yourself to that jolting moment, the very moment you were shocked. **All time is simultaneous—that past energy is still alive; you go there by thinking of it.**

It is like listening to a song on the radio which reminds you of a certain time. You can take yourself back in time to the energy of that song because the energy is still very much alive. If you bring yourself back to that jolting moment and allow yourself to stay open this time, to process out the trapped energy, then that energy block can be released.

We are energy. All energy carries a vibration, and that vibration is communication. It goes out into the universe through the law of attraction. It brings us more situations, circumstances, and events. If we keep getting things we do not want or that are in contrast to what we want, then it is time to look at who the attractor of it is. We are all attracting everything in our lives; we are creating our reality. Most people might say, "I didn't attract that; I wouldn't have wanted to create that."

Well, of course, you did not, but the energy block, from a time you do not even remember or have not thought of in decades, is the vortex drawing it in. Even if you have buried it deep, it keeps attracting things to you. You can reverse engineer it. If you do not like what is happening on the outer level, look at where it connects energetically to what is happening on the inner level. Once you release that, you are no longer attracting those things.

It would be nice if we could set our energy for joy for the rest of our lives and just be open, but it is not like going to college, getting a diploma, and you have it forever. It is something we have to work on all the time as human beings. There are many things we have to do to maintain our health. We have to drink and eat regularly to fuel our bodies. We know we have to eat because we would not live otherwise. We know we have to drink and eliminate because it's literally uncomfortable in our bodies if we don't. Yet, most of us are not aware of the energy mastery part of it.

We can fuel ourselves just by asking and feeling ourselves in receiving mode. The first couple of times may seem unfamiliar: *Close your eyes and ask for the energy you need. Imagine a waterfall of light dripping down your entire body, inside and outside of your body. Allow yourself to resonate with that energy of joy, or purpose, or whatever you choose to call it. Then become familiar with it.*

It is as if you were tuning a radio station, tuning up your energy body.

There are many ways to raise your vibration. You can bless the water you take into your body. (There's a whole study of this in the book by **Emoto**, *The Hidden Messages in Water*.) When you charge water, it creates a higher vibration, so when you are blessing it, you are drinking that in and uplifting your energy body. **When you are eliminating, you can imagine all the toxins, all negativity, all thoughts you do not want leaving with it. You can bless your food.** Moving your body even just twenty minutes a day not only helps you biochemically, but it also helps your energy. You become more connected and release the resistance of much stress. Find an exercise that you love doing for twenty minutes, even if it is walking your dog, and **while you are exercising, keep fuelling your mind with positive thoughts.** These are ways that you can increase your vibration, work with your own energy, or collaborate with a healer. There are many processes people have these days. Even reading an inspiring and uplifting book helps. On the other hand, stimulants, drugs, alcohol, sugars, and coffee lower our vibration. Being in a negative environment around people with negative thinking also lowers our vibration. Getting bodywork done is important. (I get a massage every week; I love doing things that feel good and which help to raise my energy.)

Another wonderful way to raise your vibration is to consciously say thank you. Many people do their gratitudes from their heads.

It must be said from the heart. You can list five things you are
grateful for, but to really have an impact, you need to feel it. What
helps me go deeper is listing five things about each thing on the list.
For example, I say I am grateful for my husband, and then I explain
five reasons why. I am grateful for my husband because he's so sweet
and kind. I am grateful for him because he is sexy. I am grateful for
him because he is such an amazing dad. I wish I had him as a dad,
because he is just such an amazing dad and partner, in the way he takes
care of my parents, in the way that he loves to cuddle and be so
affectionate. Do you feel a difference between listing versus the
reasons why I am grateful for him?

The fun thing about being a committed person is walking through
your own experience and teaching others about it, especially in the
form of a book. I find every time I author a book, I have to master the
contents in it and go through the deepest parts of the lessons. *The
Desire Factor* is my seventh book.

I do first-person channeling with the Quantum Council now. One
thing they always say is that any contrast that happens in our life,
whether it is extreme or not extreme, is always a gift. One needs to
look at it as a gift and not necessarily a lesson. I know many of us call
it a lesson because we are looking at it from the perspective of school;
that we go from school to school, and it is not necessarily a fun
process. When you look at it as a gift, even if you attract something
that is unwanted, it's more of a ritual. Pushing it away causes more
resistance.

I realize I must look at it and say, "Okay, like a gift, I need to open
it up, I need to unwrap it, and look inside, pick it up and interact with
the energy of this thing, because I drew it to me; it was not inserted
into my experience." So only when I open it up and feel the energy of
it am I able to release it." Then choose a different energy. That is when
it gets transmuted; that's when it truly is a gift because it's always a gift
going from resistance into freedom. Freedom is always the gift.

One of the pivotal moments of my life was when I started
channeling the Council. They always tell me that we are infinitely
loved. Each time, there is this sense of relief when I realize that I'm
loved no matter what. Even if I never do or accomplish anything
again, I am still loved. There is nothing that I could do where I would
not be loved. It is a life-changing experience when you embody that

understanding. When you realize: "Okay, I guess I can just be me then. I am just going to be loved. I will accept that love, and stop beating myself up, because I learned that it doesn't feel good. It does not feel good to be in lack, feeling like no matter what I do, accomplish, or have is never enough.

The Divine that infinitely loves you and me and all does not ever go to that place of lack. So, I do not need to go there, either.

When I was a child, we had a dial on our television to change the station. We understand now that when you switch from one station to the next station, you are switching frequencies, and because you are tuning in to a different frequency, you get a different picture.

Well, it is like that for us too if we want a different picture, if we want a different interaction in our real-life world. The things that we can see and taste, and touch and smell, and hear—if we want that to change, we have to change our emotional dial. We cannot be on the station of lack and limitation, of frustration and fear and worry, and expect to experience a life of abundance. It is like trying to watch a Western when you are on a station that has *Charlie's Angels* or you're trying to watch a movie that's not on Netflix. That is what we do all the time, because we are just not aware of our vibrations.

All energy carries a vibration—it is a spectrum or the keys of a piano. A piano has a range of keys on a spectrum of high or low tones. Imagine that these notes, tones, and frequencies represent emotions such as appreciation, gratitude, purpose, passion, love, freedom, beauty, success, wellbeing, joy and love—these are the high vibrations.

If we want to experience these emotions and how they affect our experience, we have to understand that if we are on the note of anger, that is what we are vibrating out to the universe. That is what we will continue to get in response to our energy and our vibration. Staying in anger as a set point attracts more things that push our buttons and make us angrier, because it is the same frequency and momentum. We are on that channel and have not changed it.

You have to literally change the dial, change the frequency and realize "Oh gosh, what I just said and did is in the energy of lack. I need to change the dial, to dial that up, so that I am choosing to be in joy; I am going to speak words of joy and think thoughts of joy now. I am going to joyfully expect the best to happen; I'm going to have faith that life is working out for me, and life is on my side. I'm co-creating with the Divine."

That is what we need to do to turn our dial and get on the other side of the block. It is fine if you want to attract things, like being a victim and creating victim consciousness, drama, struggle, and chaos. I did that for years. I got a Ph.D. in it, and that was a choice that I had, because I did not know any other way.

My life literally took a pivot when I realised: "Wait, what? My thoughts are not real? This limitation in my head not real?"

I have to question this thing that I have been telling myself when I realize it is not true and that I can actually choose a different thought that creates a different reality and a different feeling sense. Once I was onboard with that new energy frequency, I dove right into it and have not looked back since.

The energy of compassion takes us away from being judgmental and critical and beating ourselves up. Allow yourself to have feelings of compassion for that human moment that just happened.

Our thoughts and emotions are so interconnected, and the reason so many people stay stuck and maybe even start their journey in traditional therapy is that they're talking, talking, talking, talking, talking about how they feel, but they're not feeling and processing it out.

They are not able to isolate it from their thoughts. As you are feeling the emotions, you are releasing them. If you allow repetitive thoughts, the related emotions are going to build back up, and vice versa, right? It is not just thinking new, better thoughts; you have to do something to release the emotions as well. You cannot just say a lot of affirmations if they do not resonate with your emotions, right?

So, it works both ways: understanding that it is not all about your mindset is a huge and important part, but there's emotional intelligence too. They work in unison with each other, and you cannot do one without the other.

Why doesn't anybody tell you that? One day, you stumble upon it, and you realize, "What, wait a minute. I just lived 25 years of my life thinking that it was all about rearranging the stuff outside, I didn't know it was all about what's happening inside of me, because I was always told, 'Don't be so selfish'."

If you are selfish, you have to be self-centred, to be able to know what you are thinking, what you're about to say, how you're perceiving things, what you're expecting, what you feel, or don't feel, what action you're going to take. You have to know how to be connected enough to yourself, to be able to feel and connect with the divine life partner that each of us has.

Yet so many, especially women, are told, "Don't be so selfish; don't be so self-centred." It is interesting. Who else? Am I going to be centered on my son? I cannot be centered on my son or my husband; I can only be centered on myself. And when I am centered in myself, I feel safe, I feel expanded, I feel good, and I feel joyful. Right?

The universe lives through us, through our eyes. That divine part of us gets to experience through us individually and uniquely, and that is what is fun. We have to be centered within ourselves in order to feel the collection of energies of harmony, peace, and joy or satisfaction. Because when we feel that everybody else around us feels it, it affects everybody.

We have more to give when we are in a container of energy versus being depleted of energy, because we have brought it in, but we gave it to everybody else, and now we have nothing left for ourselves. It feels so much better when our energy is contained, and we give from the overflow. Then it is a continuous flow of good energy, and there's no lack involved.

Free 30-day Program: How to watch your words and thoughts

It is important for you to watch your words and your thoughts. The first place to start is always with your words, so I created a free 30-Day Program. It is thirty days of videos, which are short and sweet—two to four minutes in length. They tell you the word or phrase that you want to eliminate from your vocabulary, and why and what to say instead. It will help you to notice the difference when you are speaking something aloud, when you speak something that is in lack, or when you speak something that is in abundance. It starts the whole creation of a manifestation. It either creates something and births something new, or it destroys and limits what you can have and what you can do, what you can experience. It is called watchyourwords.com.

Go to www.christywhitman.com, which is my main website. I also have a podcast called *The Desire Factor Podcast*, where you can learn more about the book: www.desirefactor.com

*Special **FREE** Bonus Gift for You*

To help you live your best life

there are

FREE BONUS RESOURCES

available for you at

www.risesummits.com

For Your RISE

Enjoyed the book?

Please leave us a review 🙏

Use this link:
https://risesummits.com/amazon1

It help us get the book into more hands
and spread the message of transformation

P.S. Proceeds from the book are
donated to supporting
children in distress

Want to be featured in our next book & summit?

If you *remember* your purpose to serve others & wish to amplify your voice on a global scale. If you are ready to *inspire* people through your personal story, if you want to *share* your wisdom and *elevate* others. If you want to take your work to the next level by becoming a published, bestselling author then this project might be a great fit for you.

This project is suitable for you if:

- You are ready to increase your visibility, share your voice and your story

- You are a pioneer in the field of growth, healing & transformation

- You do your soul purpose work and currently working with clients

- You are a therapist, coach, influencer, or a spiritual leader

- You consciously participate in the transition of the planet and are actively involved in the creation of a new world

- You are ready to use the skills and tools you have learned to uplift, inspire and move people into alignment and connection with themselves

Apply here: https://www.risepublishing.net/apply/

RISE *PUBLISHING*
REMEMBER·INSPIRE·SHARE·ELEVATE

Acknowledgements

Through the years, many have shared ideas, mentoring and support that has impacted this work, each in a different way. It's impossible to thank everyone and we apologize for anyone not listed. Please know, that we at *The RISE Movement* appreciate you greatly.

Gratitude to: Ofer Lemel, Kai Lemel, Dori Kutai, Jackie Buss, Mercédes Westbrook, Vanessa Herman, Dr Joe Vitale, Lisa Cleminson Grezo, Lori Montry, Yvonne Aileen, Lion Goodman, Marci Shimoff, Dr John F Demartini, Sue Holmes, Dr Ashley Ghose, Sabine Thomas, Alena Gomes Rodrigues, Olga Brooks, Tracey Gazel, Christy Whitman, Robin Sharma, Tonny Robbins, Deepak Chopra, Dr Claire Zammit, Dr Zach Bush, Marie Forleo, Dr Shefali Tsabary, Regena Thomashauer, Oprah Winfrey, Peter A Levine, Gabor Maté, Eckhart Tolle, Brené Brown, Dr Christiane Northrup, Craig Hamilton, Ashanna Solaries, Lisa Nichols, Sonia Ricotti, Jack Canfield, Jesse Krieger, Layla Martin, Dr Sue Mortar, Brian Tracy, Dr Andrew Weil, Vishen Lakhiani, Jean Houston, Marianne Williamson, Dr Joe Dispenza, Byron Katie, T. Harv Eker, Michael Beckwith, Wim Hoff, Russel Brand, Lisa Garr, Daniel J. Siegel, Teal Swan, Mike Dooley, Dean Graziosi, James Malinchak, Amrita Grace,

Printed in Great Britain
by Amazon

81409820R00088